# Not Your Father's America

# Not Your Father's America

## An Adventure Raising Triplets in a Country Being Changed by Greed

A MEMOIR BY
# CORT CASADY

Not Your Father's America

Copyright ©2023 by Cort Casady

Published by CHANDLER PRESS
c/o Harik Thompson
25500 Hawthorne Blvd., Suite 2120
Torrance, CA 90505

www.cortcasady.com

ISBN: 979-8-9857288-0-4
eISBN: 979-8-9857288-1-1

Cover and Interior Design: GKS Creative
Copyediting and Proofreading: Kim Bookless and Monti Shalosky
Project Management: The Cadence Group
Cover Photo Credit: Curtis Dahl

All Rights Reserved. No part of this book may be reproduced or transmitted in any form or by any means, electronic or mechanical, including photocopying, recording, or by any information retrieval or storage system, without the prior written consent of the author and publisher.

This book is dedicated to Barbara, a great mom
and the best partner a husband and father could have,
and to our sons, Braden, Carter, and Jackson.
Without all of you, there would be no book
and no light so bright in my life.

# CONTENTS

PREFACE....IX

*Chapter 1*
THE FERTILITY BUSINESS....1

*Chapter 2*
PREGNANCY....27

*Chapter 3*
THREE OF EVERYTHING....51

*Chapter 4*
DIVING IN....81

*Chapter 5*
CHOICE MAN....105

*Chapter 6*
WHAT LEARNING CURVE?....123

*Chapter 7*
THREE TO GET READY....141

*Chapter 8*
TEENAGERS....161

*Chapter 9*
THE ROAD AHEAD....177

*Chapter 10*
THIS CHANGES EVERYTHING....195

EPILOGUE....213

PHOTOS....218

ABOUT THE AUTHOR....223

# PREFACE

WHEN BARBARA AND I DECIDED to have a family, we had no idea we would struggle to get pregnant, suffer the loss of a baby girl in gestation, and then face the dangers and uncertainties of a high-risk triplet pregnancy. And we had no idea that was just the prelude to a life for which nothing we had studied, nothing we had achieved, and nowhere we had been could possibly have prepared us.

Faced with the prospect of having children, I had to confront the idea of becoming a father. For me, the prospect was more than daunting. Fatherhood is something you take on for life. Once you're a father, there's no getting out of being a father. Under the best circumstances, it's fun and fulfilling, challenging and ever-changing. Under the worst, it's painful. You can be absent, aloof, a derelict, a shit-heel, or abusive, or you can be present, available, loving, encouraging, supportive, and generous. Whether your kids love you or despise you, you're still a father. You have to own it and know that being a father owns you. Having triplets took care of that.

Across the years, usually after hearing one of our amusing stories, friends would say, "You should write a book about triplets." Initially, I thought it might be interesting to write such a book. I kept a journal and notes, but then I found myself thinking, *How many parents are looking for a book about raising triplets?*

At one point, I considered writing a "self-help" book. I played with different titles: *10 Not Completely Obvious Pointers and Parables from a Father of Triplets*. Or *Life Lessons Learned by a Father of Triplets*. Or *The New Perfect: Reimagining the American Dream When You Don't Have Time to Experience It*. Or *Tips for Surviving in a Multitasking World When You're Outnumbered and Overwhelmed*. The problem was that these books weren't going to get written, because we were outnumbered and overwhelmed.

I began to realize my new and permanent role as a father was what interested me most. In addition to wanting to be an example of a good, available, loving man to my children, the other aspect of being a father that I found both compelling and worrisome was the fact that we were depositing three little souls in a world they had nothing to do with creating. At that point, I wanted to write a book that essentially would be a kind of open letter to our children. It would attempt to give them some context and perspective on the country they were born into, beyond the obvious "before Google" or "before there were smartphones." I soon realized it would need to be an extremely long letter.

What I finally decided to write, as you'll see in the following pages, is a book that combines two passions, serves two masters, and weaves together two decidedly different narratives. One, I hope, is an amusing and insightful narrative about what it's like having three kids at once. The other is a series of reflections and observations about three Americas: the one my father grew up in, the America my brothers and I have grown up in, and the America we're leaving to our children. Together, these

## PREFACE

two narratives are meant to shine a light not only on our adventure raising triplets but also on how the America we're leaving to them has changed—and not exactly for the better.

I'm glad I didn't throw away the journals and notes I kept while raising our kids. And I'm glad to have this opportunity as a father to attempt to explain to my sons the world around them as I see it. I hope you enjoy the back and forth between the two narratives and find the combination to be interesting, enjoyable, and enlightening.

*Chapter One*

# THE FERTILITY BUSINESS

> *Your children are not your children. They are the sons and daughters of Life's longing for itself. They come through you but not from you.*
> —KAHLIL GIBRAN

I met Barbara Mercer Kellard through mutual friends in October 1979. Barbara was born in Glendale, California, the middle child of three raised by Frances Chandler and Marshall M. Mercer, MD. Barb, her older sister, Marsha, and younger brother, Marty, grew up in Lancaster, California. Brilliant and beautiful, Barbara was crowned "Miss Lancaster" when she was seventeen. She was pre-med at the University of Southern California (USC) for a time then switched to UCLA, where she received a degree in design.

Barb had been married to Rick Kellard, a very funny and successful television writer with whom I had worked. Bonnie Comfort, the wife of Rick's writing partner, Bob Comfort, another brilliant comic mind with whom I had worked, introduced us. We hit it off immediately. After being together for three years, Barb and I were married in Hawaii in December 1982. We eloped. There were seven people at our wedding on the Old Pali Road at the top of Oahu: Barb, me, Mark Green, an old friend we happened to bump into on the beach the day before, the judge, a ukulele player, a singer, and our limo driver.

When I called my mother to tell her we were getting married, she asked, "Do I have to come to the wedding?" When I said no, she replied, "Wonderful. Congratulations!" My mom loved Barbara, but she had attended the weddings of three of her sons, and all were divorced, so I think she was relieved not to fly six hours to attend our wedding.

Over the next six or seven years, we used birth control. Barbara was running her own company, Kellard-Baron Designs (she uses her first husband's name professionally) one of the top five model home interior design firms in Southern California. I was writing and producing music specials, awards shows, a variety series (*Barbara Mandrell & The Mandrell Sisters*), a reality competition series (*Star Search* with Ed McMahon, the forerunner of *American Idol*), and writing songs for TV pilots.

In 1987, we decided it was time to have a family. We figured if we stopped using birth control—*boom!*—we'd get pregnant. It didn't happen. We tried everything. Barb took her temperature every morning for two years to determine when she was ovulating. We tried the "turkey baster" thing (don't ask). I had the hamster test (really don't ask). We just couldn't get pregnant.

*Fall 1990 - Los Angeles*

Then, two things happened: the bottom fell out of the California real estate market, and I was asked to produce a pilot for a possible TV series in New York. When the real estate market in California collapsed in 1990, it didn't slow down or taper off, it just stopped, forcing Barb and her partner, Beverly Baron, to close Kellard-Baron Designs in February 1991. Their specialty was designing model homes for some of the state's largest home builders. Building stopped.

While Barbara closed the doors and the books on her business, I entered a competition with two other producers to create pilots for the proposed series in New York. We each had our own hosts: I brought a gifted singer, Clint Holmes, to the competition; another producer had sports commentator Roy Firestone; the third had *Saturday Night Live* alumnus Joe Piscopo. I won the bake-off with Clint, and by October 1991, Barbara and I were living on Manhattan's Upper West Side. I was producing *New York at Night Starring Clint Holmes* for Superstation WWOR-TV in Secaucus, New Jersey, and Barbara was pursuing a drastically reduced interior design business, partly in New York but mostly in Los Angeles.

New York is where we decided to take fertility medicine to the next level.

### *Spring 1992 – New York City*

I'm holding a grapefruit in one hand and a hypodermic needle in the other. A nurse is showing me how to give another human being a shot. The human in this case will be my dear wife, Barbara. The grapefruit is a stand-in for her butt. The peel simulates the resistance human tissue offers to the hypodermic needle. The place is a fertility clinic on the Upper East Side of Manhattan. I stick the grapefruit with the needle. The nurse says it's all in the wrist. You don't push; you toss. Gently. I'm freaking out. I'm a TV writer-producer with zero medical background. This is way outside of my knowledge and interest areas, not to mention my comfort zone. After a few practice throws, I start to get the hang of it. The nurse is right—it's in the wrist. Like darts. I'll be giving Barbara hormone shots when we get back to our apartment.

I grew up the youngest of five boys. My father was a newspaper man. My mother, a former librarian, was a calm, cool, and collected manager of mayhem. I had four older brothers to look up to: Derek, who was eleven years older; Kent, ten years older; Mark, six years older; and Lance, four years older. We were all conceived the old-fashioned way. In fact, Mark,

Lance, and I were all born in McAllen, Texas, in late April and early May, so our folks must've been having some fun on those hot August nights in McAllen or across the border in Reynosa.

Let's just say it: in my father's America, there was no such thing as "fertility medicine." In fact, in the America my brothers and I grew up in, the field as we know it didn't really go public until the late 1980s and early 1990s. Point being, if it weren't for fertility medicine, Barbara and I probably wouldn't have children today. And having children is largely what this memoir is about.

Fertility medicine can be awkward to talk about and challenging to navigate. The idea is I'm supposed to give Barbara shots of hormones to stimulate her ovaries to give up her eggs; my sperm will get added to her eggs, the fertilized embryos will get transferred to her uterus, and we'll get pregnant. TMI?

I've already "donated" sperm at the clinic. They're calling now to ask me to come in and donate more. "Why?" I ask. The doctor says my sperm is "malformed." *Excuse me. Malformed? How could that be?* The doctor calmly explains that a man's sperm can become malformed by having the flu, a high fever, or a physical trauma. And then he explains that the sperm one "donates" on a given day is, in fact, made two and half months before. I did not know that. He suggests I look at what I was doing a couple of months ago. When I look at my calendar, I see that we were skiing in Utah and spending every evening soaking in a hot tub. Bingo. I donate again.

Now, it's mid-April 1992 and, after a few weeks of getting pretty good at giving Barbara shots, we're full of anticipation. It's time for the transfer. We're at the hospital. Barb's blood is being tested, and she's being prepped for the procedure when, suddenly, we're being told they're stopping. Something very wrong has developed. It's called ovarian hyperstimulation syndrome (OHSS). OHSS is a complication of in vitro fertilization

(IVF) during which a woman's ovaries swell and estrogen levels become dangerously high.

I've been administering the prescribed number of shots, but Barb has produced so many eggs that there's already too much estrogen in her system. The doctor explains that if she becomes pregnant at this point, her estrogen level will increase even more, which could be life threatening. They're not going ahead with the transfer. All the shots, blood tests, and ultrasound exams were for naught, and for today, the possibility of creating a baby is lost. The doctor explains that during hyperstimulation, Barb's veins will "start leaking like a soaker hose." As a result of OHSS, a woman can experience swelling, pain, nausea, vomiting, increased thirst, and, in severe cases, difficulty breathing and urinating. A soaker hose, really?

At home in our apartment on West 83rd, we nurse our disappointment and comfort each other. Two days later, Barb's abdomen is blowing up so much that she has added about ten inches to her waistline. Her body is unrecognizable. She's in pain. We call the doctor to ask whether he can give her something to reverse this. He tells Barb, "No, but you should be okay in about three weeks." Three weeks? They have all kinds of meds to make this happen and none to reverse it?

Three weeks later, Barb is still larger than usual and uncomfortable. Nonetheless, we fly to our friend Stepfanie Kramer's wedding in Aspen, Colorado, then drive to Santa Fe, New Mexico. On a warm, unforgettable night, we have dinner with another friend, Christine O'Connell, Hall of Fame songwriter Roger Miller, his wife, Mary, an old friend, and actor David Huddleston. Roger, who has been diagnosed with stage 4 lung cancer, is in fine form, hilarious and razor sharp. (We learn later that it was one of Roger's last nights out; he died five months later, on October 25, 1992, in Malibu, California.)

Back in New York, we're preparing to move back to Los Angeles. After producing 126 episodes and winning a New York Emmy for *New*

*York at Night Starring Clint Holmes,* I've been fired by WWOR without cause. An executive at the station who has been dying to take over the show ever since I was chosen to produce it has taken the reins of the series I created. It's painful and public. But the good news is I have a pay-or-play deal, which means I'm still being paid and will be paid the full amount of my contract; I just don't have to go to work in Secaucus anymore.

Our next step in the fertility business will have to wait. While the movers are trucking our stuff across country to a rented house in the Hollywood Hills, we decide to wait out our furniture delivery on the island of St. Barts in the French Caribbean. Good call.

## November 1992 – Back to New York

As 1992 comes to an end, Barb has fully recovered from hyperstimulation, and I've recovered from the exhaustion of producing a live TV show five days a week and being fired for the first time in my life. We're happily ensconced in a brand-new house in Laurel Canyon that the builders have been unable to sell because the real estate market is so horrible. We can see Joni Mitchell's house from here.

We still have frozen embryos at the fertility clinic back in New York. So, even though we're now living in LA, we decide to fly to New York for an IVF transfer, stay in an apartment at the Pierre generously provided by one of Barbara's clients there, and check in at the clinic. This time, we've done the hormone regimen in Los Angeles prior to coming to New York for the procedure. While Barb rests at a slight angle to encourage the fertilized eggs to nest properly, we enjoy Macy's Thanksgiving Day Parade from our high perch at Fifth Avenue and 61st Street.

Back in LA, we find out the transfer didn't work. We're not pregnant. Our hearts sink.

*March 1993 – Los Angeles*

Roughly four months later, we're trying again, this time in Los Angeles. Our fertility doctor is Dr. Joel Batzofin, who has a busy practice in Pasadena. His name is pronounced "*Bats often.*" Really? Yes. A fertility doctor who bats often. That's what you want. "*Scores often*" might be better, but we immediately love him.

Based on our experiences so far, Joel decides to do an exploratory laparoscopy and, in the process, remove some scar tissue holding down one of Barb's fallopian tubes. Apparently, Barb's fallopian tubes, which are supposed to act like a pool sweep, have not been sweeping her eggs from her ovaries into her uterus for implantation. Removing the scar tissue may solve the problem. And it occurs to me only a guy engaged in fertility medicine in the '90s would describe a fallopian tube as a "pool sweep." Not in my father's America.

Understanding that Barbara's sensitive to medications, given the hyperstimulation in New York, Dr. Batzofin prescribes a much lighter hormone regimen. Nonetheless, Barbara produces an unprecedented thirty-eight eggs. Joel says when he asked one of his colleagues to guess how old his patient (Barbara) is, his colleague says, "Twenty-seven, maybe twenty-eight." (Barb's 43.) This time, Joel recommends a GIFT procedure which, because I know you're wondering, stands for gamete interfallopian transfer. This is where our gametes—Barb's eggs and my sperm—are injected together into a fallopian tube via another laparoscopy.

It works. Within a few weeks, we find out we're pregnant. Amazing! By the way, I'm clear that *I* won't be pregnant, but we use the royal *we* in the pregnancy business. After more than six years of trying every other means possible, this one worked. We're excited.

Twenty-one weeks later, on July 10, a heartbreaker. We're losing the pregnancy.

We're at Cedars Sinai Hospital in Los Angeles. Barb's in early labor, and they can't stop it. She delivers a tiny baby girl, born alive, heart beating but without the lung capacity to live for more than about thirty minutes. A nurse suggests Barb hold the baby so she can know she's real, know she existed, if only briefly. At first, Barb resists, thinking it's too morbid, then she relents. She holds the baby on her chest for as long as she can. I hold Barb. We name her Angie.

Losing Angie is devastating beyond anything we could imagine. In my mind, I already had her in high school. I had imagined so many experiences we would share together as father and daughter. Suddenly, it's all gone, never to be.

Barb falls asleep, and I fall asleep on a rollaway bed in her hospital room.

The next morning, I wake up into a deep sense of grief and sadness. But it's not just because of our loss. Suddenly, I feel profoundly connected to my friend Rocco, whose daughter was murdered years before when she was in her early twenties. Our experiences are completely different. And yet I have a feeling I'll never forget—a powerful, singular, shared realization that we're all connected by our humanity and, in this case, unbearable loss.

As the weeks pass, we're in a fog, in the grip of grief.

We know a miscarriage is an experience that can either bring a couple closer together or tear them apart. As excruciating as it is, fortunately, our loss, our grief is bringing us closer together.

Barbara says, "I keep asking myself, why me? Why us?" Then one day, she says, "Today, I realized that even if God herself appeared and gave me an answer, it wouldn't help; it wouldn't change anything. So I'm going to stop asking that question."

It's the beginning of healing.

Jennifer Butler, a friend who lives in France calls and says we should come visit; she insists. She has suffered a similar loss and says where she lives is a healing place. So we pull ourselves out of the house, out of our gloom, and burn through the last of our AAdvantage miles to fly across the world. In a foreign country, we must contend with the language, local customs, taxis, currency exchange, high-speed trains, shopping for food, a borrowed car, and driving ourselves around on strange roads. We're getting out of our heads; we're getting back into life.

After ten days in France, we fly home through New York, where we're greeted and comforted by dear college friends. We're finally getting past it. Not over it, just past it.

*November 1993*

Back in LA, working at our jobs and feeling thoroughly discouraged about our prospects for creating a family, we're out of time and money. Our friends, Bonnie and Bob Comfort, have generously given us $3,500 for another turn at bat. We attempt another IVF transfer, this time using frozen embryos stored at the doctor's clinic in Pasadena. This is the same procedure we flew to New York for a year ago.

Didn't work in New York. Doesn't work now either.

It's starting to look like we won't have a family. Even though the clock is ticking, we're not able to deal with any more loss. We need a break, some time to do our careers and have the experience of making something happen. As two people who have run successful businesses, succeeded at big jobs, and felt reasonably accomplished in life, we're feeling helpless and defeated in the fertility business. We keep trying, and we get our hopes up, only to have them dashed, procedure after procedure. My Writers Guild health insurance has been covering our fertility expenses, but we've burned through the $25,000 cap and are on our own. The costs are mounting. We're worried about the outcome: Is this ever going to work? Are we ever going to have a family? And I'm worried about how we're going to pay for all of it. While I'm pondering the latter, I realize the best thing I ever did was become a member of the Writers Guild of America (WGA).

When I joined the WGA in 1979, I had no idea how important it would be to have medical insurance. I was young and healthy and didn't need it. Now, in November 1993, as we struggle to start a family, I appreciate that without my union's insurance coverage, we couldn't afford fertility medicine.

I joined the Writers Guild in order to keep working as a professional television writer. The Guild negotiates with television networks, movie studios, and producers on behalf of all writers to establish the minimum amounts writers are to be paid for their work. In an industry where writing is too often undervalued and, generally speaking, writers are not their own best representatives, the work of the WGA has been transformational. By far, the most important benefit of being in the Writers Guild is quality health insurance that travels with you from job to job throughout your career and into retirement.

The first TV show I ever worked on was called *The American Flyer*, hosted by Dan Rowan, best known as cohost of the classic late-'60s TV series *Rowan & Martin's Laugh-In*. The format for *The American Flyer* was inspired by the success of television's first primetime news magazine, *60 Minutes* on CBS. I got hired because I had been a freelance magazine writer. One of the stories we did was about a young comic named David Letterman; another was about an intensely ambitious young Austrian bodybuilder named Arnold Schwarzenegger who was trying to break into show business. I didn't have to be a member of the Writers Guild to work on that first show. Under the Taft-Hartley Act, I was allowed to work on one union show without being in the union. Then, if I wanted to keep working, I had to join the union. After *The American Flyer*, I paid the initiation fee and became a union man.

I grew up with a positive impression of unions and respect for union workers who, across many industries, were the backbone of the America I grew up in. Unions were respected—until 1980, when President Ronald Reagan, often referred to glowingly by our Republican friends as "the greatest Republican president" (I thought that was Abraham Lincoln), launched a relentless, unwarranted attack on unions in America.

Ironically, even though Reagan had been president of a Hollywood union called the Screen Actors Guild (SAG) and had received the support of the Teamsters Union, the Airline Pilots Association (APA), and the Professional Air Traffic Controllers Organization (PATCO) during his 1980 campaign against President Jimmy Carter, Reagan was the first president to engage in union busting. One of his first acts in office was to crush the Professional Air Traffic Controllers Organization (PATCO) like a bug on the windshield of his limo. When air traffic controllers went on strike for better working conditions, better pay, and a thirty-two-hour workweek, Reagan declared the strike a "peril to national safety" and ordered the controllers back to work. Historically, presidents didn't interfere in union business. Such matters were left to the companies or the government and union representatives.

When only 1,300 of the nearly 13,000 air traffic controllers returned to work, Reagan fired all 11,345 of the striking controllers who ignored his order and banned them from federal service *for life*. (The ban was rescinded by President Bill Clinton in 1993.) In the wake of the firings, it took the FAA years to recover. But damn it, Reagan showed those good, all-American workers who was boss, and he set the tone for how Republicans would treat unions for decades to come—as the enemy.

As a newspaper editor and publisher, my father had a contentious relationship with unions. He was part of management and had to negotiate with unions throughout his career. Historically, the most powerful union in the newspaper business was the International Typographical

Union (ITU) of the United States and Canada. The ITU was one of the oldest of the traditional American Federation of Labor (AF of L) fraternal craft unions in the country. It was absorbed by the much larger Communications Workers of America (CWA) in 1987, but during my father's time, the ITU was all-powerful. He negotiated with the ITU when he was running the newspapers in Brownsville, Harlingen, and McAllen, Texas, in the 1940s and Phoenix, Arizona, in the 1950s. They were tough negotiations for him, partly because he was under pressure as a member of management to hold the line on union wages and partly because he fundamentally believed unions were a good thing. In my father's America, unions were ascendant.

Like so many people at the end of their life, my father struggled with short-term memory loss. He said it was the result of "cardiovascular antiquity." We would have lunch and, a few minutes later, he couldn't remember what kind of sandwich he had just eaten. But if I asked him about union negotiations with the ITU, his recollections were crystal clear.

In today's America, unions are under attack and in decline. Antiunion forces on the right have portrayed them as being bad for America. Following in Reagan's footsteps, conservative Republican legislators around the country have pursued a determined, coordinated effort to pass state laws that take away the bargaining rights of teachers, first responders, nurses, and other unionized workers. They've gone after *teachers* because teachers are organized. Citing the cost of their salaries and pension plans, they've gone after firefighters and police officers, hotel workers, and state, county, and municipal employees for having union representation and collective bargaining. After all, we wouldn't want to overpay teachers and first responders the way we do CEOs. But another reason conservatives want to destroy unions is because of politics, not policy. They fear the solidarity that unions create among workers and the money they can pour into progressive political campaigns.

## May 1994 – Last Chance

In mid-May, after a six-month break, Barbara is willing to give fertility medicine one more try, and so am I. If we strike out again, she may want to throw in the towel and the needle and the hormones. As we discuss which procedure to do, Joel recommends we go for inserting the embryos in the fallopian tube, since that's how we got pregnant before. Only this time it's a ZIFT procedure. The difference between GIFT (what "we" had before) and ZIFT is that with GIFT, the sperm and egg (gametes) are put in separately, albeit at the same time, and fertilization takes place in the fallopian tube. With ZIFT, the gametes are combined first in a Petri dish and inserted as a zygote, already fertilized. An embryo comes from a zygote. On the bright side, we still have some frozen embryos left. At one point, we had twenty-six frozen embryos – the equivalent of the extended Osmond Family, the Jackson 5, and the Flying Wallendas, all on ice.

Dr. Batzofin says patients like us are called "the walking wounded" because we've suffered so many losses, including losing a baby in gestation. For the ZIFT procedure, Joel tells Barbara he wants to thaw out one cryogenically frozen "straw" containing embryos for the transfer. He says each straw holds five or six embryos. Enough to duplicate the Jackson 5 plus Janet. But the survival rate on defrosting is around 50 percent—this is a numbers game, remember—and Dr. Batzofin hopes to get three or four viable zygotes after defrosting.

The day before the procedure, Joel calls to say that the embryologist thawed out one of our straws containing five embryos instead of one with six. Three survived. Joel asks Barbara what she thinks. "How many did you want?" she asks. "Well," he says, "we prefer four embryos, hoping to get one to take." They agree to go with three and hope for the best.

The day of the procedure, I drive Barb to Pasadena for an exam at the doctor's office then over to Huntington Hospital for the transfer. Joel wishes us luck and shows us a lucky silver dollar he carries for good measure. Barbara has a silver dollar in her purse, which she drops into the pocket of his smock. I'm wishing I had a dollar to give to his bookkeeper to apply to our bill.

Huntington Hospital is great. The lobby looks more like a Four Seasons Hotel than a hospital. And I'm figuring the bill will look like the Four Seasons too. As we go through admissions, we put $3,000 on a credit card, a down payment on a hospital bill that's going to be north of $12,000. We're committed. I deliver Barbara into Dr. Batzofin's expert hands, pray that he'll hit a home run, and return to work.

That afternoon, around three o'clock, I pick up Barb. She says the procedure went well. But in the fertility business, they don't just tell you it went well; they send you home with a video of *exactly how it went*. That evening, as Barbara rests, we watch the video. It's the damnedest thing. I want to call it *Voyage to the Center of Barbara*. The pictures are astonishing. I think it needs music, but it's great. We travel in through the wall of her abdomen via an optic fiber with a light and a camera on the end. Suddenly, we're inside! In a pink, white, and orange soft tissue universe, we're getting a guided tour from the doctor: "There's the left fallopian tube," he says, sounding more like a golf commentator than a doctor. "Don't want that one ... it's tied down with white, spider-webby stuff ... scar tissue ... there's the right fallopian tube ... looks good ... there's the bowel ... back to the right tube." Into the picture comes a catheter. After a couple of attempts, the catheter is inserted into the fallopian tube and, before our very eyes, we see a little globule moving down the catheter and disappearing into the fallopian tube. Voila! Zygote interfallopian transfer. ZIFT.

All we have to do now is wait. Rest and wait. In a month, we'll know if "we're" pregnant.

Later, Barb tells me about a conversation she had with Dr. Batzofin to which I, the husband and potential father, was not a party. It seems that by the time she got to the hospital, only *two* of the original five embryos had survived the defrosting, and Joel felt he needed to thaw another straw. Sounds like a country song I promise not to write:

*HE WASN'T SURE JUST WHAT TO DO*
*BUT HE KNEW JUST WHAT HE SAW*
*AND THE ONLY WAY TO GET THIS DONE*
*WAS TO THAW ANOTHER STRAW*

Joel and Barbara agreed.

So, on doctor's orders, the embryologist thawed another straw. This one contained *six* embryos *four* of which survived. Dr. Batzofin put the original two and the four new survivors into Barb's right fallopian tube. At the time, I was driving home from Pasadena listening to Garth Brooks.

### June 9, 1994 - A Birthday Present

We're celebrating Barb's birthday at La Valencia Hotel in La Jolla. Old Hollywood charm, new Hollywood prices. A few days later, back in Los Angeles, Barbara has a blood test. The results are positive.

She's pregnant.

### July 1, 1994 - The Moment of Truth

Four weeks after the transfer, we return to Dr. Batzofin's office in Pasadena for an ultrasound. The three of us are in the examination room. Joel applies some warm jelly to Barb's belly and moves the wand around in search of life. We see hazy images on a TV monitor. I'm good with this. I work in TV. I like seeing images on a screen, even when I don't know what they are. The wand stops on a shadowy shape in what looks like a cocoon. Joel says it's an embryo. We see a tiny pulsing group of cells and hear a rhythmic, high-pitched sound. "That's a heartbeat," he explains. "T-cells doing their early work." Awesome.

"Well, it looks like you're pregnant," Joel says with pride. Barb and I look at each other and smile. Joel moves the wand around some more and comes to *another* embryo containing a tiny cluster of pulsing cells. "Looks like you've got twins," he says. Silently, I'm thinking, *Twins would be cool. Two kids in one shot, and we're done.* Barbara looks at me with dewy eyes. I figure she's thinking the same thing or having an allergic reaction to the lubricant on her belly. The doctor moves the wand around some more and comes to *another* embryo with a "heartbeat."

"Well, well . . ." he says cheerfully. "It looks like you've got three!"

"Wo. Hold your phone!" I gasp. "Go back! I think that's the first one."

"No, no," he says, moving the wand around again. "Look . . . here's one . . . two . . . and number three. You could have triplets," he says with a big smile. He's elated. His statistics just shot up. Our hearts just stopped.

This is *not* cool. We ordered one Happy Meal, not a Family Picnic. I'm scared. I look at Barb. Her dewy expression has turned to deer-in-the-headlights. She's surging with hormones-times-three scared. We can't believe this is happening. We're going from being a couple on our way to dinner to a *party of five*. Overwhelmed. Silence driving home.

I thought this was supposed to be high-tech fertility medicine—as in, you get what you want. We were hoping to get pregnant with *one* baby. Although it's been a year, losing little Angie at twenty-one weeks in a labor and delivery is still fresh and painful. We're terrified of going through that again. And a triplet pregnancy is a high-risk pregnancy. God help us.

*July 4, 1994*

Three days later, we're arriving at Barb's family picnic in Irvine, California. I think it's the fifty-fifth annual Fourth of July Mercer Family Picnic. For years, the Mercers have had two reunions a year, one on Christmas Eve and one on the Fourth of July. For a while there, I was afraid they were going to be arrested for over-gathering. Anyway, somehow the word has leaked out that Barb's pregnant—four weeks or six, depending on when you start counting. We haven't mentioned triplets. We've been told there's a fifty-fifty chance in a triplet pregnancy of losing the whole thing in the first trimester. So we're not being specific. We're just waiting to see what happens.

*July 7, 1994 – Laurel Canyon*

I'm thinking about my mother, Virginia. She died in 1987, and the moment she passed, a flock of doves flew out of the tree outside her room. She was a great mom, and she would have been thrilled to know we're pregnant. She loved Barb. If only she could be here to help us with our family, however big it is. But we won't have Virginia, and we won't have Barb's mom, Frances, either. She passed away unexpectedly when Barb was only twenty-one. I wish I could have known her. Barb's father is alive, and so is mine, so if we do have children, they'll have two grandfathers, for a while.

*July 8, 1994 – Pasadena*

Driving back to the fertility clinic in Pasadena for another ultrasound exam, I wonder whether nature will get us out of this gracefully. We're told that, frequently, the body eliminates one of the embryos. Natural selection. A woman's body is built for one. Right? Fingers crossed out of fear.

The ultrasound tells a different story: the three fetuses are firmly in place and now, with the vestiges of three vital heartbeats, it's obvious they are viable embryos. We have triplets in the making.

The exam is followed by an uncomfortable conversation with Doctor Joel in his office. He tries to do his job and inform us of both the risks and joys of having multiples. "The important thing to think about is how many children you want," he offers. "It's like a tree. Don't think about the branches and leaves yet. Think about the roots, the trunk. Think about whether you want three kids or not."

*I'll tell you what I'm thinking about,* I say to myself. *I'm thinking about suing you for putting too many embryos in my wife.*

"If you don't want three kids," Joel continues, "then you can consider having a reduction," a euphemism for eliminating one of the fetuses with a chemical injection.

We're about to face the toughest decision of our lives.

We stop for lunch at Il Fornaio in Pasadena, struggling to understand our situation. I order a glass of wine. Barbara's not drinking. I'm drinking and staring into space. We don't know how to deal with this.

We meet with the first of several perinatologists. Perinatology is a subspecialty of obstetrics concerned with the care of the fetus and complicated, high-risk pregnancies. After discussing our history, we ask about reduction. The doctor won't commit. He says his success rate with triplets is such that he thinks we'll be fine if we go ahead with three. We drive home saying little, staring out the window a lot.

Over the weekend, we see friends—the Glazers and the Haydens—and we tell them we're pregnant. But we don't tell them Barb's pregnant with triplets. We may elect to reduce this pregnancy, and we sure don't want to go blowing it around that we had three and reduced to two.

Next stop, UCLA. To meet with another highly recommended perinatologist, an expert when it comes to multiples. We've been warned that this doctor's patients frequently must wait for *two hours* to see him. This doesn't make him our pick, but we need his advice.

Sure enough, we wait for two hours and fifteen minutes, along with others, very pregnant others, who are logging similar wait times. This guy has more wide bodies in a holding pattern than O'Hare Airport during a snowstorm. We're wondering, *Is he clueless or just completely insensitive?* We're getting steamed. I finally step up to his receptionist to complain. She offers a lame excuse: "Oh, he had an emergency and is running behind." I had to stop her from perpetuating what even *she* knew was a lie. "No," I said, "we know the story. We were told to expect this. Everybody knows the wait times here are insane. The question is *why*?" She looks at me with a blank expression. She has no answer. She's just trying to keep the moms from going ballistic, going home, or spontaneously delivering in the office.

Finally, we get in. The doctor is attentive and knowledgeable, a very reassuring guy with a lot of experience. He seems to have no idea that he has kept us and 90 percent of his patients waiting for more than two hours. Later, I figure it out: either his receptionist uses an appointment calendar where you can schedule appointments every fifteen minutes, or she can't stand it if there's an empty chair in the waiting room. The doctor, on the other hand, being a good, caring doctor who spends time with his patients, is working on an entirely different paradigm.

Eventually, after an ultrasound exam, reviewing Barb's history, and discussing our lost pregnancy last July, Dr. Makesuwait, we'll call him, comes closer than anyone to recommending that we "reduce" the pregnancy. From three to two. He would never recommend reducing to one, he says, because if there were any chromosomal abnormalities detected in a later amniocentesis test (Down syndrome, for example), you'd have the option of reducing one fetus and keeping the other. Good point. Statistically, he says, the data isn't definitive on the risk of having triplets versus the risk associated with reducing from three to two. But when pressed, the good doctor says he thinks we should reduce, leaving the decision to us.

## July 19, 1994

*Tick-tock.* Next, we drive out to Pasadena to see Dr. Marc Lebed, perinatologist number three. He looks like Paul Simon. Barb likes him. He spells out all the risks of proceeding with a triplet pregnancy very clearly but doesn't recommend a reduction. That would be up to us. We both think he would give us great care.

Among Dr. Lebed's recommendations to mitigate one of the most common dangers of triplet pregnancies—early delivery—is to take one baby aspirin each day. We're shocked. We've read that aspirin can be dangerous to pregnant women because it can increase the risk of bleeding in the brain of premature infants. Turns out Dr. Lebed participated in the studies on this and, in small doses, one baby aspirin a day can help stave off hypertension (toxemia), a leading danger to the mother in multiple pregnancies because it can cause a stroke. The only treatment for toxemia is to deliver the babies early in order to save the mother's life.

Later the same day, we meet with psychologist Rona Schwartz. We were referred to Rona when we lost Baby Angie. Thoughtful, caring, and insightful, she helped us through our grief. Now, she's counseling us as we struggle with whether to reduce or not. We're testy. Feeling intensely emotional about the possibility of a reduction, Barbara's comparing our situation to *Sophie's Choice*, the powerful movie starring Meryl Streep in which a mother is forced to choose which of her two children to give up to the Nazis. I think the analogy is a little over the top. How am I supposed to reason with that? Besides, I'm still pissed off at Dr. Batzofin for putting in so many embryos. As I've complained out loud many times, I thought this was Designer Baby Time. We didn't order three. We ordered one!

Hello? I haven't said this to Barb but, secretly, I don't see why we don't reduce and get on with it. Rona does—she's reading Barbara—and I'm learning that pregnant women are a force all their own. Barbara's afraid of the choice. I'm afraid of the future; I don't know how we're going to afford to raise three children at once.

As we leave Rona's office, I'm thinking about fatherhood—not in the abstract but in terms of what it may be like for me, very soon. And I'm thinking about my father. He and my mother raised five sons with eleven years between us. How did they do it?

In my father's America, folks lived on what they made. That continued to be true in the America my brothers and I grew up in, until the 1970s and 1980s. We lived in an *income-based* economy. If you got a promotion at work, maybe you could move to a bigger house or a better neighborhood. For the most part, people didn't lease or finance cars. They bought the kind of car they could afford. You rented a house until you could afford to buy. As a rule of thumb, your housing expense was supposed to be no more than one-quarter of your income. If you made $125 a week, you could afford an apartment that cost $125 a month. At my second job out of college, as a production assistant on the *Smothers Brothers Comedy Hour*, I made $125 a week, and my apartment on Orange Drive was $125 a month. Perfect. It was 1969.

The way my brothers and I were raised, your standard of living was based on how much the breadwinner of the family earned, and there was usually only *one* breadwinner. In our house, my father was the breadwinner. My mother raised us five boys—a huge job that paid nothing. Later, my mother became a real estate broker to pursue a personal passion and add to our family's income. More about her later. Together, they borrowed some money to buy the newspaper my father published for a decade, but that was a business investment.

So here I am, in 1994, working in my chosen field as a television writer-producer. Barbara's an interior designer. We're a DINK couple—Double Income, No Kids—and we're doing fine with two incomes and no kids. Then I look up the estimated cost of raising *one* child born in 1995 to the age of eighteen in California, not including extracurricular sports, music lessons, college tuition, and room and board, and it's $145,000. Times three is $435,000, and it's going up fast.

I have a reasonably fertile imagination, but I'm having trouble imagining how we're going to come up with an extra $400,000 to $500,000 over the next eighteen years just to raise our family. Maybe it's possible, but I can't see it right now. Unless we go into debt.

Speaking of debt, I've had an American Express card since 1965. I know. Talk about respect. You should hear how they treat me when I call AmEx customer service. "I see that you've been a member for over fifty years, Mr. Casady. And you're still alive?"

I received my AmEx card when I was a sophomore in college. I was a full-time student with a part-time job. There was no way I qualified for a credit card. But one day I received an offer in the mail from American Express to apply for their card. My older brother, Kent, who happened to be in town and had a good job, agreed to cosign my application. The next thing I knew, I was a "member" and, as they used to say, "Membership has its privileges." That was before "Don't leave home without it." Or today's slogan, "Don't *live life* without it." Getting an AmEx card was my initiation into using credit to live on, and it coincided with the transformation of America to a *credit-based* economy.

In 1994, as we face the prospect of having three children all at once and what it will cost, the opportunities to borrow seem far greater than the opportunities to earn. How are working families like the one we're hoping to become making ends meet? I discover, for example, that, according to the Economic Policy Institute (EPI), despite low unemployment in 1994, "The typical American family is working more hours, is taking on historically high levels of household debt that far outpace small stock market gains, and often fails to receive adequate health care and pension coverage from their employer." Meanwhile, according to the EPI, "The real wage of the median CEO rose 62.7% during 1989-99, helping the typical CEO to earn 107 times more than the typical worker." Remember, we're in 1994 and, since 1978, CEO compensation has risen 940 percent while American workers have seen an increase in compensation of 11.2 percent. (Source: *The State of Working America*, Economic Policy Institute, August 31, 2000.)

Borrowing on credit cards has exploded to the point where, in 2020, Americans had an estimated $444 *billion* in credit card debt. This is according to Social Finance, Inc. (SoFi), an American online personal finance company. SoFi "provides student loan re-financing, mortgages, personal loans, investing and banking services to a growing customer base seeking to leverage their lives," which means *going into debt*.

At the same time, roughly a fifth of Americans "have zero or negative net worth," according to *Forbes* magazine and, as you read this, the numbers are likely even worse. "If left unchecked, wealth will continue to accumulate in fewer and fewer hands, a trend we've been witnessing for decades," the EPI concludes.

The nation's "Gini Index," which was developed by Italian statistician Corrado Gini in 1912 to measure income inequality, has risen steadily over the last four decades. During that time, experts say that 82 percent of the gains in wealth have gone to the top 5 percent of Americans, while 43 percent of the gains in wealth have gone to the top *1 percent* of earners.

Oh, and the US Department of Agriculture estimates that, by the time our children reach the age of ten, the cost of raising a child to the age of eighteen in California will go from $145,000 to $233,000 each.

The numbers are mind-bending. And disturbing. In the summer of 1994, as a father-to-be, I'm less concerned with the disparity between the überrich and the rest of us than with losing financial control of our life. I'm a freelancer, meaning after one job ends, I don't always know when or if another job will come along. Fortunately, over the past fifteen years, the work has been remarkably consistent. But now, faced with the prospect of raising three children simultaneously, I feel less certain. Plus, we're still deeply enmeshed in our quandary—three or two?

*July 21, 1994*

To the degree we can, we're seeking comfort in relationships with family and old friends. We're getting together for dinner with Dr. Mark Weiss and his wife, Marilyn, who are longtime friends and the parents of triplets. They didn't find out Marilyn was pregnant with three until she went for an amnio test at sixteen or eighteen weeks. The nurse turned to her and said, "How much do you know about your pregnancy?"

"Not much," Marilyn said. "I just know it feels different than the last one."

The nurse said, "Excuse me. I'm going to get your doctor." The doctor broke the news and Marilyn turned as white as the paper covering the examining table.

We used to delight our friends by telling the Weiss's story. They already had two older kids around eleven and thirteen. They were done. Then, while they were on vacation, they saw a couple with a baby and decided to have another kid. This was *before* fertility medicine, so they were gobsmacked when they had triplets.

When we heard the news that the babies were born, we went to visit. Actually, we went to offer our sympathies and see the sideshow. Sure enough, we were stunned to see three cribs, three highchairs, and three babies. Mark and Marilyn were overwhelmed but graceful in their exhaustion. We pitied them. We thought it was totally nuts. On our way home, we laughed out loud about how crazy their situation was. "Poor Mark and Marilyn," we said. "What were they thinking? They're screwed!"

Now, years later, over dinner, as we explain the choice we must make to reduce or not reduce, a fascinating thing happens. Marilyn, the mother of triplets, says if she had the option, she might reduce.

"They're a lot of work," she warns. "It's been tough on Mark. It's dangerous and expensive."

Interestingly, Mark says the opposite. He thinks we can do it. "Don't be ridiculous," he says. "Have all three! It's wonderful."

Opposing opinions in one marriage. Go figure. After dinner, we ride back to the Weiss's house in two cars—Marilyn with me in the passenger seat of our Explorer and Barbara with Mark in their car. Mark and Marilyn are great friends, not only because they both agree and disagree but also because they're willing to be at our side through this process, to listen and offer their support no matter what we decide. They are loving, compassionate, understanding, and fun.

*July 22, 1994*

We meet the head of perinatology at one of the area's leading hospitals. Barbara notices he's wearing a goofy tie. Again, we ask for advice on whether we should attempt to have triplets or not. He won't commit. He says the risks are greater, yes, but with proper management, it can be done successfully. He refers us to one of his colleagues.

A few days later, we meet with his colleague. The guy looks like he's right out of central casting: fifty-something, gray hair, distinguished face, a gentle, pleasant demeanor, no goofy tie. He's saying he thinks Barb can have triplets, assuming we want them. Out of an abundance of caution, he recommends she be checked for an infection of the cervix which, if present, could result in complications and may have been the cause of losing Angie. He says Barb should drink massive amounts of fluids and make a practice of lying down on her left side twice a day for thirty minutes, from the very beginning, which is *now*. Lying down on the left side, he says, increases blood flow to the babies and can have a significant impact on the outcome and how long Barb is able to carry them.

*July 28, 1994*

I'm having lunch at Morton's in West Hollywood with my old friend Glenn Padnick, a college classmate, president of Castle Rock Entertainment and the "father" of the hit TV series *Seinfeld*. He's about to go away on summer vacation. Glenn and Eleanor have three kids ages ten to eighteen, so they're old hands at the pregnancy and parenting business. He orders iced tea. I order wine and break the news: Barb is pregnant with triplets.

Glenn offers an unexpected observation. He says he loves his kids, all of them. But he has the most fun when he's with just *two* of them. It doesn't matter which two, he says, the oldest and the youngest, the youngest and the middle one, just so long as it's *two*. He loves all three, of course, and sometimes he's with all three. But it's about the attention he can give to two, not three. It's about the way two are together without the third. It will be some time before we experience the fundamental truth of this insight. I think, *Oh jeez. How are we ever going to pay attention to three at once?*

We have a great talk. Glenn says he's sure we'll do the right thing. I mention that after all my years as a freelancer, I suddenly feel the need to get a *real* job. Something steady. I'm actively looking for work.

Glenn says, "You mean a fifty-two-week-a-year job?"

"Yeah."

Chapter 2

# PREGNANCY

> *Trust yourself.*
> *You know more than you think you do.*
> —DR. BENJAMIN SPOCK, PEDIATRICIAN

In the silence surrounding my fear of the future, I'm thinking about my father again. About how, when I was seven years old, my dad got fired by a man named Eugene Pulliam.

After managing three newspapers in the Rio Grande Valley of Texas where I was born, my father became the editor of the *Arizona Republic* and the *Phoenix Gazette*, the morning and afternoon newspapers in Phoenix, Arizona. It was 1950. He was forty-two years old. His boss, Eugene Pulliam, was a wealthy and influential publishing magnate and the head of Central Newspapers Inc., which owned more than a dozen big papers including the *Republic* and *Gazette*. I once asked my mother what Mr. Pulliam was like, and she said, not joking: "He cheats at canasta." I thought that was hilarious and terribly telling.

Many years later, Pulliam's grandson, Dan Quayle, became vice president under George Herbert Walker Bush (Bush #1). Mr. Quayle became famous for saying dumb things like, "I believe we are on an *irreversible* trend toward more freedom and democracy—but that could change."

Anyway, one day my father—we called him "Pop"—was fired by Gene Pulliam because, among other things, Pop ran a story in the paper about then Vice President Richard Nixon having a political "slush fund" that Nixon was allegedly using for personal purposes. Every newspaper in the country was playing the story on page one. Mr. Pulliam, a staunch Republican, wanted Pop to bury the story in the back of the paper, but he wouldn't do that. "We're a newspaper, Gene," he told Pulliam, "and this is news." Pop also got crosswise with Mr. Pulliam over the behavior of "an insubordinate executive" at the paper who I believe was Mr. Pulliam's nephew. So Pop got fired.

Determined to become his own boss, my father and mother drove to California in search of a small newspaper they could buy. Imagine that. It was every newspaperman's dream to own his own paper. They drove from the top of California to the bottom, from Eureka, near Oregon, to Chula Vista, near the Mexican border, stopping in every little town and hamlet that had a small independent newspaper that was or might be for sale.

They found the *El Cajon Valley News* in East San Diego County about thirty freeway minutes from the beach and about an hour from Mexico. I know. Too bad about the beach. I guess the *La Jolla Light*, in one of California's premiere beach towns, wasn't for sale. The paper was a "shopper" that came out twice a week on Thursdays and Sundays, and they could afford it. They paid $65,000 for the *El Cajon Valley News*, using money they had saved and some they borrowed. My father achieved his dream—he became the editor and publisher of his own newspaper. He got a piece of the American dream right there. It was 1954.

Almost immediately, my dad set out to expand the *Valley News*, as it was also called, into a *daily* newspaper. He built a new building, bought a new printing press, and purchased composing machines, including some that had been damaged in a fire. He hired reporters, photographers, typesetters, proofreaders, pressmen, advertising salesmen and women, a circulation manager, job printers, and paperboys. He created jobs. He didn't get any special tax breaks to do what he was doing; he just did it. He was turning a twice-weekly paper into a daily.

Did I mention it was 1954? When my mom and dad were growing the *El Cajon Valley News*, the maximum federal income tax rate on regular income was 91 percent. That's right, 91 percent. My father wasn't complaining about the tax rate. He was growing a business, one that would serve the community and support our family for the next decade.

Growing up, I heard the old saying, attributed to Benjamin Franklin in 1789: "In this world nothing can be said to be certain, except death and taxes." I got it. Taxes came with the territory. They weren't *evil*. They were *inevitable*. They were part of life. Politicians didn't swear a pledge that they'd never, ever raise taxes. That would've been like saying they were never, ever going to die.

This notion that taxes are *evil*, and we shouldn't have to pay them, is a relatively recent perversion advanced by a guy named Grover Norquist since the mid-1980s. Grover grew up rich. His father was a vice president of the Polaroid Corporation which, when I was growing up, used to make "instant" cameras. (Amazingly, they still do.) You could take a picture with a Polaroid and, in minutes, a *color print* of the photograph you had just taken would come out the front of the camera! It was (and is) astonishing.

Around the age of twelve, the story goes, Grover came to believe that taxes were *evil*. I grew up not-so-rich and came to believe that taxes were a necessity, that they were the price we all have to pay to enjoy the country we live in.

My family never belonged to a country club, and nobody I knew growing up belonged to a "gym." I think some of my older brothers' friends worked out at the YMCA because the "Y" had a gymnasium. And there were gymnasiums at high schools. But in the '60s, people didn't join gyms and work out. They smoked and drank, as you know if you've ever watched *Mad Men*. Today, of course, we know quite a few people who belong to country clubs, even more who have gym memberships, and hardly anybody who smokes. They gladly pay their dues to be members of their country clubs and gyms and don't think much of it.

But when you think about it, why should anyone have to pay dues to use a country club or a gym? Why can't you just go in there and use the exercise equipment, swim in the pool, play golf, and use the tennis courts for free? It's there. Why should you have to pay to use it?

Because if you didn't, there wouldn't be a country club or gym. There'd be an empty lot with weeds on it. The gym or country club wouldn't exist for you to use if *someone* didn't pay for it. And that someone is you. In the America my father left to me, we understood this. I thought everybody understood this.

Taxes are like dues, or better yet, membership fees. Taxes pay for all the things we all get to use—roads, bridges, schools, airports, dams, water systems, sewer systems, the power grid—things that wouldn't be there if we didn't all collectively pay for them. Taxes also pay for all the people who make our lives better and safer: teachers, first responders, city planners, postal workers, sanitation workers, the army, navy, air force, marines. Taxes are an *investment* in what we want and need to function as a country.

Painting taxes with a big, black brush, the way Grover Norquist has, is called "framing," which is a twenty-first-century term for spinning the truth or, more accurately, distorting it. Instead of "framing" taxes for what they are—the membership fees we pay to enjoy everything we all need and share—taxes have been framed as an excessive unnecessary *evil*, especially for the rich. "We should be able to keep more of our money instead of giving it to the government," the anti-tax zealots say. I tried this with the gym. I told them I was going to keep more of my money instead of giving it to them. They said, "Fine," and locked me out of the gym.

My father and millions of entrepreneurs like him were able to create jobs and grow businesses when the tax rate was 91 percent and 60 percent and 40 percent. Pop boosted the reputation and circulation of the *El Cajon Valley News* by making the paper bigger, by serving advertisers better, by joining the Audit Bureau of Circulation (ABC) to confirm readership, and by giving readers a robust, alternative editorial policy. And he supported our family for ten years, including sending my brothers and me to college on what he made from our family-owned business.

My point: My mom and dad had five kids when Pop lost his job in Phoenix, and somehow they made it. They got brave and creative and resourceful and figured out what they needed to do to keep a roof over our heads, put food on the table, and have a professional life they could be proud of. They were probably scared sometimes, but they soldiered on. And importantly, in the mid-1950s, they were able to make a go of it; they were able to buy and grow a business, create jobs, and dutifully pay their fair share of taxes, because America was a country in which reaching and thriving in the middle class was still possible.

Pop sold the *Valley News* in 1964 for roughly a million dollars. The federal long-term capital gains tax rate at the time was 25 percent. Without a complaint, he wrote a check to the US Treasury for $250,000 and dispatched my eldest brother, Derek, to deliver it to the local IRS office.

### *July 1994*

We're meeting frequently with Rona, our therapist, who's trying to help us through the Triplet Dilemma. I'm stuck! Life isn't going the way I wanted it to. By using fertility medicine, we're messing with Mother Nature anyway, so why can't we get what we want? That's what life is about, isn't it? Getting what you want?

*Think again, Bosco. Time to grow up.*

Barbara's good at reminding me that thinking we're in control of our lives is an illusion. She would know. She's caught in the emotional and hormonal vice of motherhood. No kidding. She says she's willing to let me make the decision. If I think we should reduce the pregnancy, she says she'll go along. But she wants to be out cold for the procedure. She wants me to knock her out at home with a rag soaked in chloroform and deliver her to the hospital. Really? No. She said that, but she was kidding. It's clear to me that she no longer wants to talk about reduction. And it's starting to dawn on me: hormones and a mother's instincts are not about to let her mess with this pregnancy.

On the drive home from the therapist, a lot of emotions are surging in the front seat. We're polarized. I feel like Barb's trying to force her will on me; she feels like I'm trying to force my *fear* on her. As we pull into the driveway and I turn off the engine, Barb spots something on the floor and picks it up.

"Whose fingernail is this?" she says accusingly, holding out a tiny red thing.

"I don't know," I stammer, leaning in to get a closer look.

"Well, it's got red polish on it, and I haven't been using nail polish since I got pregnant!"

Fingernail? Red polish? Where did this come from? I feel like we're in the Twilight Zone. A minute ago, we were disagreeing about a major turning point in our lives, now it feels like I'm being accused of infidelity.

The next day, I figure out the Mystery of the Red Fingernail. I tell Barb that the nail must belong to Marilyn Weiss, who rode in the front seat of the Explorer the night we all went out to dinner. She was wearing red nail polish! Barb says she already concluded the same thing.

## PREGNANCY

*August 5, 1994 – The Precipice*

At our next appointment with Rona, not much has changed. It still feels like we're on different sides of this precipice. It's not that I want to reduce the pregnancy; it's that I'm scared. We can see the other's side, but we're not changing our positions. Rona does her best to mediate and soothe.

That night, we call our friends, Jane and Jerome Downes, two of the most expert, experienced, loving, powerful, accomplished, and transformed people we know. They're leaders of the Landmark Forum, a remarkable program for personal and professional growth that we've both taken, so we're good graduates, good listeners, and open to coaching. They agree to advise us on how to get through what we're now calling the Swirling Vortex of Thorny Issues. One of the exercises they recommend is called the Fear Process, where we sit down together and share our fears about having triplets. Oh boy. Can't wait.

*August 13, 1994 – The Fear Process*

Barbara and I are at the Writers Guild Theatre in Beverly Hills with twenty or thirty minutes to kill before a screening of *The Client*. We decide it's a perfect opportunity to do the Fear Process exercise. It's a simple process. One person says what they're afraid of. The other person just listens. No comments, no reactions. Just listen. Then the other person goes. After we look at our fears, we're simply supposed to decide what we're committed to doing.

I go first, listing all my fears: Barb will become so large that she'll look like a Shar Pei dog and never get her body back, and she'll hate me for it; she'll have some complication during the pregnancy and die; the kids will be born premature and have learning disabilities; we won't be able to handle three kids by ourselves and won't be able to afford help; we'll be totally taken over by the kids and lose our relationship with each other; Barb will be in bed for months and I'll have to wait on her; as the youngest of five, I'm used to getting attention and, with three babies, I'll never get any more attention. Then, Barb shares her fears. They're astonishingly similar. She's afraid she will lose her shapely body; she's afraid of hypertension; she fears a miscarriage; she fears losing our relationship; she's afraid the kids might have learning disabilities. Without realizing it until now, we've been looking at the same issues, fearing the same things. It's the beginning of a breakthrough. And the movie's starting.

### August 17, 1994 – Pop's Birthday

We're driving to La Jolla to celebrate my father's eighty-sixth birthday at a party with my eldest brother, Derek; his wife, Nancy; my brother Kent, and an assortment of friends. It's not unusual to have time to think on the 405 Freeway. It can take two hours or four hours to get to La Jolla, depending on traffic.

I'm remembering that FBI Director J. Edgar Hoover thought my dad was a communist. Pop always suspected this and confirmed it many years after he retired. When he received his FBI file through a Freedom of Information Act (FOIA) request, the file confirmed that the Bureau had been surveilling my dad for years; they clipped and filed dozens of his editorials about Hoover and the Vietnam war; they even planted someone in our midst who regularly played tennis with my father. I found out about this guy one evening when he showed up at our family dinner table. He obviously liked my dad; he enjoyed playing tennis with him; he used to take photos of our family when he came around which, for some reason, didn't arouse suspicion. The strangest thing was he didn't seem the slightest bit embarrassed when we found out that he was spying on Pop the whole time. The creepy part for me was he kept looking at me and saying, "You were such a golden boy."

The birthday party is great. No creepy spies. Just family and close friends. In the past few years, Pop has lost his short-term memory. It's not Alzheimer's. He seems very present, but he has difficulty recognizing old friends and acquaintances. This is especially frustrating for a man who is well-known and can't remember those who remember him.

One day, we were in the car. Pop was driving in his neighborhood, not far from my parents' house. We pulled up to a stop sign and sat there a little too long. Finally, Pop turned to me and said, "Which way do I turn? I can't remember." I told him to turn right, and he did.

Then he looked at me and said, without apology, "You know, this happens more and more. I'm fine once I get going, but I'm not sure sometimes which way to go."

I asked him, "When that happens, does your mind wander?"

He thought a moment and said, "No. It just *stands still*."

At one point during our birthday visit, when Barbara and I are sitting with Pop, without being specific, we mention that we're facing a big decision.

"Don't worry," he offers. "Whatever you decide, you'll look back and realize you did the right thing." It was profoundly reassuring, as only a father can be.

Later in the evening, my dad is sitting at the end of the table set for fourteen, just happily waiting for dinner to be served. He's still incredibly handsome. Tall, slim, with white hair and a mustache. I decide to give him his birthday present before dinner. I figure he and I can enjoy the moment together and, his memory being what it is, if we want to give it to him again later, he'll enjoy it then too.

He opens the box. It's a plaid shirt we thought was just right for him. He looks at me, his eyes wide like a kid and says, "For me?" I nod. He really likes it. Thanks to Barbara, it's a perfect color on him.

Later, during dinner, I'm looking at Pop while he's eating, and I'm struck by something truly remarkable. I see the much younger man inside his eighty-six-year-old exterior, full of youthful energy, peering out through octogenarian eyes. It was stunning. I thought about us possibly having triplets and wished my father was younger, like the man I could see inside. Pop loved kids. In recent years, he allowed his housekeeper, Juana, to raise her four children under his roof. I wish our kids could know Grandpa Simon. I wish he could take care of them. Then I think, maybe not. He's so forgetful, he might misplace them.

*August 18, 1994*

The morning after Pop's birthday, Barbara and I are heading out to have breakfast with Derek and Nancy before driving back to Los Angeles. As we leave the hotel, Derek calls to say Pop has fallen in the bathroom. When we get to the house, the paramedics are there. Suddenly, he looks frail and vulnerable to the perils of old age. We follow the ambulance to the hospital where x-rays reveal he has broken his femur. He'll require surgery and will be recovering for months.

*August 25, 1994*

We're out to dinner with Steffanee and Louis J. Horvitz at Talesai on Sunset Boulevard in West Hollywood. Louis J is a big time TV director with shows like *Live Aid*, the *Oscars*, the *Grammys*, and the *Kennedy Center Honors* to his credit. We've been working together making outstanding television shows since the mid-'80s. Barbara and I must be getting used to the idea of *three*, because we tell Steff and Lou we're having triplets. They almost pass out.

*September 12, 1994 - Coping*

We're having a social dinner with Dr. Batzofin and his wife, Diane, to get better acquainted. Joel's worried that I hate him. I don't, but I enjoy making him uncomfortable. I tell him that, if we have triplets, I'm thinking about suing him for support of the *third* child. It'll be a landmark case. The dinner is very enjoyable, and Joel picks up the check. I'm not hating him as much.

After interviewing six of the top perinatologists in Los Angeles, only one recommends a reduction; the others are basically saying a triplet pregnancy is doable. We decide to work with Dr. Marc Lebed. He impressed us with his informed, matter-of-fact approach and his attention to managing the details. The process has been arduous and emotional. Whereas the miscarriage brought us together, we're bouncing back and forth between what we simultaneously know is a blessing and the fear that it could be a disaster, as we struggle to make our decision. We're beginning to realize that there's no "right" decision; there's just the decision we will make.

Still, fear is my constant companion. Back in the late 1980s, when we were still a DINK couple, we participated in a personal growth and awareness program in Santa Rosa called "The Six Day." It included classroom work and a ropes course with a fearsome zip line.

By fearsome, I mean I'm standing on a board about five hundred feet above a canyon floor, and the zip line probably runs three or four hundred yards out and down to the bottom. My legs are shaking. The attendant hooks me to the line twice, main and safety. I tell him, "My legs are shaking." He says, "It's a good thing you don't have to hang on with your legs." I'm so scared I can hardly swallow. He says, "Grab the bar over your head and step off the board." Really? And possibly plunge to my death? That's counterintuitive. But I do.

I'm freefalling. My stomach is in my throat. Then, I'm rocketing down the zip line, and it's utterly thrilling. An exhilarating, heart-pounding, soul-liberating ride. When I get to the bottom, I feel free and enlightened in a way I've never felt before.

Here's what I learned: I was afraid. I trusted the team, the harness, the integrity of all the safety measures, but everything about stepping off that board was terrifying. And I understood that my fear wasn't going to go away. All there was to do was *include it* and take it with me.

The Fear Process that Jane and Jerome Downes have recommended is about *including* our fears, not trying to deny them. And by acknowledging and including our fears, we have a breakthrough. All there is to do now is ask ourselves, *What are we willing to take responsibility for?*

To "reduce" the pregnancy, we had been advised to do it between twelve and fifteen weeks. We're now at sixteen or seventeen weeks. Barbara never felt good about reducing the pregnancy. She couldn't bring herself to do it, and if she couldn't, neither could I. I respect her decision completely. It's our decision now. We've decided to be responsible for having triplets and for whatever may come with a triplet pregnancy. We're clear: we are taking responsibility for the three souls that the universe is entrusting to us.

*September 16, 1994 - The Day of Reckoning*

Barbara is having an amniocentesis procedure at eleven o'clock in the morning with Dr. Lebed. During an "amnio," an ultrasound wand is used to show the position of the fetuses in the uterus on a monitor. A sample of amniotic fluid, which contains fetal cells and chemicals, is withdrawn using a long hypodermic needle and submitted for testing.

In the amnio room, Dr. Lebed spends thirty minutes to locate and identify each fetus—maternal right, center, left. Each has its own placenta. He examines each fetus, looking for any outward signs of abnormality. He's very precise and thorough. Everything looks good.

He pierces Barb's abdominal wall with the needle and intrudes into one of the amniotic sacks to remove a small amount of fluid for testing. Barb must lie completely still, even as the pain from the first needle makes her want to jump off the table. I'm watching the doctor, Barbara, and the monitor, mesmerized.

After drawing the first sample, Dr. Lebed injects a small amount of inert blue dye to mark where he's been. Methodically, he does number two and number three.

Dr. Lebed's concentration is palpable. He's razor-focused yet calm. I'm wondering if the experience is as intense for him as it is for Barb and, by extension, me. When he finishes with number three, he pushes back on his rolling chair, peeling off his gloves and releases a guttural sigh. He looks completely drained.

"Triplets are never easy," he whispers.

The procedure has gone perfectly, and it has taken Dr. Lebed's years of experience and powers of concentration to do it.

Now, we wait ten days to get the results. We'll learn the sex of each fetus, their chromosomal makeup, whether any of the three are at risk for Down syndrome, which ones will get into Harvard. If all three are healthy, we're committed for the long haul. The only reason to reduce now is if, God forbid, one of the fetuses is abnormal.

Welcome to the triplet pregnancy business.

*October 12, 1994*

Still searching for a fifty-two-week-a-year job. Met with Michael Douglas at the Peninsula Hotel in Beverly Hills to discuss opportunities in the emerging multimedia business. I've known Michael since 1987 when he purchased an original screenplay of mine, and we met several times to discuss it in New York and LA over the next two or three years. (Films take forever to get made. Mine didn't get made.) Michael's very cordial, as usual. When I mention that Barb's pregnant with triplets, he flips. He's really pleased and excited.

*November 1994 – Growing Babies*

Barb's a great patient, which is very important because ours (hers) is a highly managed pregnancy. Here are the ground rules: She takes pregnancy vitamins and one baby aspirin each day. She has to lie down on her left side for thirty minutes *twice* a day. No alcohol. No coffee. No hair coloring. No fingernail polish.

Later in the pregnancy, at the end of every day, Barb has to lie on her side in bed with a belt around her belly that's connected to a wire that's plugged into our phone. The belt is a monitor that picks up contractions, even tiny ones, and sends the information over the phone to a monitoring station in Pasadena where technicians keep track of Barb's condition.

All's well until late November. After one evening session, the phone rings. It's Dr. Lebed's office. "You've had two contractions," the nurse says. "Dr. Lebed wants you to go to the hospital."

Barb doesn't want to go. "I thought the deal was two or less," she says, "and I've only had two."

"The doctor insists," the nurse says.

I take Barb to Huntington Hospital, where she spends the night. When I pick her up the next morning, she's wearing a Terbutaline pump which dispenses small doses of the anti-contraction chemical night and day. Turns out that going to the hospital overnight was pretext for fitting Barb with this device.

The pump would be noticeable if Barb wasn't pregnant. But on a pregnant woman the size of Poughkeepsie, it's hardly visible. Barb is enormous. From behind, she looks pretty much the same. But swing around sideways and it looks like she's carrying a 28-inch Sony TV. The old tube-type.

Nonetheless, she's feeling reassured and well cared for. The last thing we want is for her to go into premature labor. A normal pregnancy is forty weeks. With multiples, the average is thirty-three and half weeks. "We" need to get to there.

While I keep trying to find a "real job," Barbara continues to follow doctor's orders: lying down on her left side, getting monitored every day, growing three babies, all while pursuing her interior design business. She's been an interior designer for twenty years. For the first ten years of our relationship, she was building a company that became one of the top design firms in Southern California, creating the interiors of model homes for some of the state's largest home builders. Kellard-Baron Designs had fifteen employees, occupied four thousand square feet of office space and two thousand square feet of warehouse space, and was responsible for helping to market more than $2 billion worth of residential properties in West Los Angeles, Malibu, Huntington Beach, Palos Verdes, Moreno Valley, and other Southern California communities. It was the kind of business that woke Barb up in the morning and dragged her out the door to work.

When we first started trying to get pregnant, I dreamed we had a baby, and I went to Barb's office one day with our baby. In my dream, the office had a little nursery, and Barb and all the women in the office were playing with the baby. When I shared the dream with Barb, she looked at me, paused, and said: "I can't imagine that at all." And then she went out the door to work.

Barbara is an award-winning member of the American Society of Interior Designers (ASID) and masterful at what she does. Still, the transition from running a big company to working with one associate and a bookkeeper has been challenging. Now that we're back in Los Angeles, she's continuing her design business on a smaller scale with a much lower overhead, a higher profit margin, and much less stress. All while being pregnant with triplets and, periodically, dealing with morning sickness.

It's inspiring to watch Barb navigate working while growing our family. She has clients in the Pacific Palisades area of Los Angeles who want her to design their new eight-thousand-square-foot residence. Barb's up for it, but she wants to make sure they are. She tells them she's pregnant with triplets and says, "If you want to use another designer, I will understand completely." They stay with Barbara and remain clients to this day.

In West Hollywood, there's a building where interior designers go to look at fabrics, furnishings, carpets, wallcoverings, tile, you name it. It's called the Pacific Design Center (PDC). It's a massive place skinned with blue glass, housing dozens of showrooms on several floors. Locals call it "the Blue Whale."

One day, a large Barbara, pregnant with three babies, is at the PDC with her design associate, Vicki Poole, looking for fabrics for a client. As they enter one of the showrooms to make selections, Barbara collars a sales associate. "Is anyone using that desk chair?" she asks pointedly. When the salesperson says no, Barb immediately appropriates the chair, which has wheels, and pushes herself along the fabric wings, making selections as Vicki takes notes.

"I'm pregnant," she explains, gliding away.

Barb says there were times in the past when she was at work, especially when she and her team were installing model homes for an opening night, when she felt "completely on purpose." She enjoyed the feeling of being clear about what she was supposed to be doing and then doing it. Now that she's pregnant, she says she feels on purpose *all the time*, innately confident that she's doing exactly what she's supposed to be doing every minute of the day. She loves how she's feeling.

I come home from work and ask, "What did you do today?"

Barbara answers, "Today, I grew thirty fingers and thirty toes."

### November 18, 1994 – Mark

My brother Mark, an agronomist, six years older than I am, died today of valley fever in Bakersfield, California. A great loss. His ex-wife, Linda, their son, Justin, who lives in Japan, and I all had a chance to visit Mark in the hospital in the weeks before he passed. We all knew the end was near. Mark had symptoms for some time but ignored them.

When Linda calls Justin in Japan with the news—sometime Friday evening California time, Saturday morning in Japan—Justin says he just finished telling his girlfriend, Seiko, about a dream he had, around the time Mark passed. Mark appeared before him all dressed up and said, "Justin, I'm going to die." Justin said, "But, Pop, you look great." Mark said, "I know, but I'm going to die, and everything is going to be okay." When Justin told his mother about the dream, she understood instantly. Linda had shared experiences like this with Justin before, but he never believed her. Now, he finds himself saying, "Mom, I never would have believed it if it hadn't happened to me."

I was able to say goodbye to Mark and to thank him for being a great brother. Mark was the best politician in our family, a true friend, and a wise advisor. At one point early in my career, when I wanted to move from the "business" side of show business to the "show" side to become a writer, Mark told me, "Don't try to change in front of people. You need to unplug, make the change, and then plug back in." That's when I left Hollywood, moved to Sun Valley, Idaho, for a year, then to San Diego and started writing—scripts, songs, and magazine articles. I came back three years later as a writer to "plug back in" to what would eventually become a long career in television, film, and music. Thank you, Mark. You are remembered and missed.

### *November 24, 1994 – Showered with Love*

A group of our friends is throwing a baby shower for us. Not the kind where a bunch of ladies sit around drinking white wine and oohing over baby things. This is a "couples shower." This is a party. The hosts are my niece, Wendi, a realtor; commercial singers Kathy and Steve Coon; actors Deborah May and George DelHoyo; Barbara's design partner, Vicki Poole, and her medical malpractice attorney-husband, Mitch Roth; TV program distributors Jennifer and Jim Hayden, who have a six-month-old girl of their own; and Marilyn and Mark Weiss, the parents of triplets who have been our North Star and are graciously hosting this affair.

The Weiss triplets—Ryan, Lizzie and Sarah—now ten years old, are bringing us the presents, helping us unwrap the abundance of gifts, carrying away the wrapping paper, keeping track of who's giving us what. Wait! Did Steffanee and Lou Horvitz just arrive with a high chair? (They did.)

The evening is overflowing with love and laughter, friendship, and music. May the blessings never end.

*December 24, 1994*

Christmas Eve in a triplet pregnancy. We'll never have another Christmas Eve like this one. Barb's pretty much "on bed rest" from here on out, other than "one easy outing" per day. In the evening, we drive through a torrential rainstorm to Barbara's annual Christmas Eve family reunion. As we visit, dine, and share presents, Barb is warmly celebrated for her size and the miracle of this pregnancy. I'm so proud of her.

*December 25, 1994*

Christmas Day. It feels like the greatest presents we'll ever receive are on their way. We spend the day resting then venture over the hill to our dear friends Susan and Barry Glazer's Christmas party, another "easy outing." Barry is one of the most talented and enduring directors in television—funny, charming and a total pro. Dick Howard, my former William Morris agent, is there. So is Stu Billett, who created *The People's Court*, and a lot of other show business friends. As always with the Glazers, it's a lovely affair. Barb parks herself on a lounge chair and says she'll probably want to leave around 10:30 p.m. Pregnant women know things. At 10:25, we're in the car.

*December 28, 1994*

Our twelfth wedding anniversary. We have a romantic anniversary dinner at the Bel Air Hotel. Barbara abstains. I drink for five. I give Barb a silver clock like the one we gave each of the couples who cohosted our baby shower—a small memento of the fabulous years we've spent together and a keepsake for what we're about to experience. After dinner, we join two friends, "JG" and Don Caverhill in the Bel Air's classic bar. Don wrote the hit song "Louie, Louie." They treat me to a fine cigar and a Scotch. Barb's having water. All in all, a lovely, quiet celebration.

*December 31, 1994 - New Year's Eve*

It's the quietest New Year's we've ever spent. Barbara's in bed. At 11:55 p.m., she rolls over on one side. At ten minutes after midnight, she rolls over on the other side. That's it. That's our New Year's Eve.

I'm wondering how far a woman's body can expand. Could she explode? I ask Dr. Lebed, "If I accidently bump into Barbara with a safety pin, could she explode?" He answers as any professional would: "Please hang up the phone, Mr. Casady. I have work to do."

While I worry for both of us, Barb's being a great patient and things are going well. God only knows what lies ahead in 1995.

*New Year's Day, 1995*

The daughter of our dear friends Anne and Marshall Goldberg calls to remind us about an afternoon party we said we'd attend. We forgot. It hasn't occurred to us to go out today, not even for an easy outing. We're staying in bed.

*January 6, 1995*

Barb's been taking it easy for almost two weeks now. My niece, Wendi, is taking her to a regular, scheduled check-up with Dr. Lebed in Pasadena. He says he thinks she'll go at least another two weeks. Afterward, Wendi and Barb go to breakfast. When Barb gets home, Anne Goldberg arrives with Chinese food. Barb's not hungry but she loves Anne and enjoys their time together.

Meanwhile, I'm sitting in for late-night TV talk show host Tom Snyder as his crew runs through two "shake down" shows before they launch his CBS series. Great fun. The test shows are mostly for the director and tech people to get up to speed so things will run smoothly when Mr. Snyder sits down to work. Nonetheless, the producers want these to be "real" shows. So the talent producer, Carole Propp, the dear friend and colleague who got me the gig, is tasked with getting "guests" for me to interview. Carole asks Barb whether she would be willing to come in and talk about our situation. Barb says yes, not realizing that she'll be coming off a full day at the doctor, breakfast with Wendi, and a visit with Anne.

Unbeknownst to me, after Anne leaves, Barb is left to shower and gingerly get dressed by herself. The show sends a car to pick her up. She arrives looking great, and I'm interviewing her about being pregnant with triplets, focusing mostly on the technology and the medicine, not fully realizing that she's in the umpteenth hour of what amounts to *three* "easy outings." Barb says that toward the end of a pregnancy, you understand that things are happening to your body over which you have no control. You can feel nature doing its thing. "You realize," she says, "you're just along for the ride."

I figure this will be a great piece of video to have. One day, the boys will get a kick out of watching Mom and Dad talk about their imminent arrival. I thank Barb for coming in, Carole puts her in a car that will take her home, and I interview the next guest.

*January 7, 1995 – "I feel different."*

From the minute she wakes up, Barb complains about feeling achy. During the 4:00 p.m. monitoring session, she has a couple of contractions and is asked to monitor again. She must lie perfectly still so the monitor doesn't send a "false contraction" over the phone line. The nurse tells her to monitor a third time, which makes Barb even more cranky and uncomfortable. The nurse tells her to increase the medication dispensed by the T-pump. While they're talking, Barb tells the nurse, "Today, I just feel different." The nurse immediately orders us to go to the hospital. Now. We find out later that "I feel different" are *The Words* pregnant women say when they're about to give birth.

It's 5:45 p.m. Barb is lying down on the backseat of the Explorer under two seatbelts, wincing with pain every time we hit a bump. I drive the thirty minutes to the hospital with tremendous care and intention. I hate that she's in pain, but I can't do anything about it. We arrive at Huntington Hospital in Pasadena at 6:15 p.m.

After Barb's admitted and examined, the nurse tells her she's dilated to three centimeters. A short time later, her water breaks. We've been at the hospital for forty-five minutes. I'm so glad this didn't happen at home. Or in the car. If it had happened at home, we probably would have freaked out and gone to Cedars Sinai Hospital, which is closer to home but where nobody knows us. Being here is much better.

*Delivery*

Our lives are changed. The Casady Triplets are being born between 8:00 and 8:26 p.m. after thirty-three and a half weeks in gestation. They're early but not too early. Actually, they may be the first Casadys in history ever to arrive *early* for anything.

The scene in the delivery room is beyond comprehension. As planned, the babies are being delivered by Cesarean section (C-section), so Barbara is lying on an operating table, sedated, with an epidural for pain. Two doctors are attending. Sadly, Dr. Lebed, our lead physician, is at dinner and unable to make the delivery in time. Dr. Bryan Jick is filling in expertly. There are also six neonatal nurses in the room, two at each of three "crash carts" for the newborns. I'm sitting in a chair wearing blue scrubs from head to toe, including a head cover and booties, witnessing the scene as best I can without getting in the way.

Within minutes, the doctors deliver Baby A, handing him to one of the neonatal nurses who promptly carries him to cart number one for instant assessment in the form of an Apgar score. The Apgar is a measure of the physical condition of the newborn. It is calculated by adding points (2, 1, or 0) for heart rate, respiratory effort, muscle tone, response to stimulation, and skin coloration. A score of 10 represents the best possible condition. I'm getting up and crossing to cart number one. All I can see are the nurse's eyes.

"Is he okay?" I ask. They wipe some blood from his mouth and make their assessment. The nurses nod and give a thumbs-up. Their eyes say he's fine. Not even a minute has passed.

The doctors are handing Baby B to the nurses from cart number two. I cross to them. Baby B cries; the nurses give a thumbs-up. He's fine too. Another minute.

I can't believe it. I can't believe where we are, what I'm witnessing, what Barb is doing, what the doctors and nurses are doing. I'm overwhelmed.

Baby C is tiny, which worries me, but he's crying, and the nurses' assessment is positive.

As Dr. Jick prepares to close Barb up, he turns to me and says enthusiastically but also as kind of a warning, "These ovarian tubes look good!"

Foolishly, I stand up to look—why, I have no idea—and what I see is my wife's belly laid open. I nearly faint. Note to self: don't look over there anymore.

Suddenly, the crash carts are moving, and before I can say, "Which way is the bar?" Barbara, the doctors, nurses, carts, and babies are gone. I'm standing in a long hospital hallway, wearing blue scrubs, a head cover and booties, with no idea where to go or what to do next.

All I know is I'm a father of three healthy baby boys.

Eventually, I find out that Baby A, born at 4 pounds, 14.5 ounces, is being taken to the neonatal intensive care unit (NICU) because he had blood on his face and they're concerned he may have inhaled some.

Baby B, weighing in at 4 pounds, 12 ounces, is headed to the regular nursery.

Baby C, tiny at just 3 pounds, 11 ounces, is headed to the NICU with Baby A to receive special attention because he's under four pounds.

It's a relief to be out of the nerve-racking, nail-biting pregnancy business. But it's daunting to realize that what's next is a lifetime in the parenting business.

It's also daunting to find out the hospital bill for the birth of the triplets is well into five figures.

Chapter 3

# THREE OF EVERYTHING

> *Everyone should have kids. They are the greatest joy in the world. But they are also terrorists. You'll realize this as soon as they're born, and they start using sleep deprivation to break you.*
> —RAY ROMANO, ACTOR AND COMEDIAN

The hospital is telling Barb they need to discharge her. The nurses are saying that her hospital stay is up, and an orderly keeps asking when she'll be giving up the room. Feeling incredibly pressured and upset, she calls me then calls the insurance company; I call the insurance company; Dr. Lebed calls the hospital. A C-section is major surgery and with a major surgery, the mother's body needs time to heal. In the back and forth with the insurance company, a woman finally comes back to Barbara and says, "Okay, we've agreed that you can stay another day, but Baby B [who's in the regular nursery] needs to go home."

"Excuse me. You're a woman, right?" Barbara asks. "And you want to send my preemie baby—who's nursing—home without his mother? Are you kidding?" Then it occurs to Barb that it's just about the money. "I'm staying, and we'll work this out later," she says. The next time the orderly asks about the room, Barbara says, "I'm not going, and the baby's not going without me."

(Nowadays, thanks to legislation passed the year after we had our babies, mothers who've had a C-section can expect to stay in the hospital for three to four days after delivery, longer if there are complications. The Newborns' and Mothers' Health Protection Act of 1996—the "Newborns' Act"—prohibits hospitals and insurance companies from limiting length of stay after childbirth to less than forty-eight hours for a vaginal delivery or ninety-six hours for a caesarean section. The final set of regulations went into effect on December 9, 2008.)

*January 9, 1995*

Meanwhile, I've hired a baby nurse to show us what to do after Barbara and the babies come home. And right now, I'm at Toys "R" Us with a shopping list from the nurse for everything from burp cloths and mittens to bottles, pacifiers ("binkies"), and crib blankets. This is my first official act as a father: buy all the little essentials you need when you bring a baby—or in our case, three babies—home from the hospital.

I walk into the store knowing nothing and ask to see the manager. I explain my situation and beg her to help me. She's busy and wearing a telephone headset, but she's sympathetic and agrees to be my Sherpa. She looks at the list and says, "You'll need three of everything." I realize she has just named the "show" we'll be doing for the next eighteen years.

I follow her, pushing the largest market basket known to man. We're about to pick out blankets when my lifesaver looks at me and says, "Excuse me." Then, speaking into her headset, she chirps: "Good afternoon, Toys "R" Us. How may I help you?" She listens then presses a button on the transmitter pack she's wearing on her hip.

"Plush toys on one. Plush toys on one."

Her voice booms over the store's PA system. She turns back to me, glancing down at my shopping list, unfazed. She throws six blankets in the basket, explaining we'll need at least two blankets for each baby. "All right, let's move on to baby bottles," she commands.

How crazy is this? This woman is managing the store, answering the phone, *and* assisting a customer.

At the cashier, all I can think is, *Three of Everything*. I buy twenty-seven items... times three... times two more in some cases... eighty to one hundred purchases... spending a fortune, taking everything home where, along with all the items we received at the baby shower, our nursery is now fully stocked.

*January 10, 1995 – Staying Dry*

The biggest storm in history is sitting on Los Angeles. Five inches of rain. There have been something like two thousand auto accidents on freeways and streets because drivers in Los Angeles don't know how to drive if so much as a leaf drops from a tree, much less if it rains. I don't dare to drive to the hospital. Instead, I drive down the hill in our four-wheel drive Explorer to pick up the housekeeper. It's like a whitewater rafting trip. The housekeeper is a no-show.

I talk to Barb on the phone several times between placing pots, pans, and wastebaskets under the various leaks in the house and arrange for our baby nurse, Gladys Flowers, to come over after Barb and Baby B come home tomorrow.

*Handwriting*

It's still raining. I interview a possible live-in nanny at Greenblatt's Deli on Sunset Boulevard. Her name is Marta. From El Salvador. She's forty-seven, has raised six kids of her own, and is available to start right away. I like her. I get a handwriting sample from her and tell her I'll call her in a day or two. She's available to start right away.

For years, Barbara and I have used handwriting analysis to screen employees. Barbara used it to hire the fifteen employees in her design business. We found out about handwriting from our neighbor in Laurel Canyon, Andrea McNichol, a leading handwriting examiner who has consulted with the FBI, the US Department of Defense, the Justice Department, Fortune 500 companies, police departments, and entrepreneurs like us. Andrea is the author of an illuminating book on the subject, *Handwriting Analysis: Putting It to Work for You.*

Handwriting analysis isn't about penmanship. Handwriting is a "brain print" that reveals 70 percent of the personality with 90 percent accuracy. You don't get results like that from interviews. Among the attributes that handwriting analysis reveals are integrity, temperament, punctuality, and discipline—all essential qualities in a person who's living in your home and taking care of your children.

We have dozens of stories about handwriting reports on people we almost hired. In one case, a woman I interviewed to be my assistant received a negative recommendation, and the examiner warned, "Be careful how you tell her you're not going to hire her. This person is dangerous." The analysis on a woman who applied to be the chief financial officer of Barb's company concluded that she was so good at accounting, but so dishonest, that she could steal the company blind before Barb knew it. In another instance, the analysis was, "Hire this woman immediately. You don't find people like this every day." That woman, Bren Dahl, turned out to be one of the smartest, most efficient, organized, and dedicated people I've ever worked with. (After working for me, Bren ended up marrying Curtis Dahl, the photographer who would take our family Christmas card pictures for twenty-one years. They're still married and dear friends.)

Knowing Barb and Baby B are coming home tonight, Deborah May, a treasured friend and an outstanding actress, by the way, drops by with chicken soup, bread, salad, cookies, and something "feminine" for Barb. Deborah's an angel. When I remember I need to take a car seat to the hospital, which we have thanks to the fabulous baby shower our friends threw for us, Deb suggests I wash the cover. Good idea. Especially since one of our cats has been sleeping in it for two weeks! She also suggests we wash some baby clothes for the baby's First Trip. I can't believe my good fortune. Where would I be without Deborah May?

At 2:30 p.m., I leave Deborah doing laundry and go to the Happy Day Domestic Agency on Ventura Boulevard in the Valley to interview more live-in nanny candidates. The girls, mostly Latinas in their twenties who are waiting in a nearby room, are brought to me one at a time and introduced. It feels awkward. One of the girls is wearing too much makeup. She looks like she's going to a fiesta. They don't speak enough English to know what I'm saying, and my Spanish is no bueno. I get handwriting samples from three. Doesn't look too promising.

It's easy to get the handwriting samples. In addition to a standard employment application, you give the applicant four pieces of white, unlined paper and a ballpoint pen. On one page, they are asked to "Write a short paragraph about your future, then sign and date the page." On another, the instruction is, "Write a brief letter to yourself, sign and date." On the third, "Please write the alphabet and the numbers 1 through 20, sign and date." And on the fourth sheet, the instruction is simply, "Draw a wheel, sign and date." An applicant who won't do this, or any part of this, is refusing to do the first thing you're asking them to do. Good to know. Next.

There are no "correct answers" in a handwriting sample. The samples produce a useful "brain print" that the examiner can analyze to assess the applicant's character and personality. It's not that you're looking for "perfect people" or "the perfect hire." It's about knowing who you'll be working with, what you can expect from them, how they're likely to behave, and how to manage them. It feels right to use this tool to screen the individuals who will be literally holding our children's lives in their hands.

## Going Home

When I get home from the nanny agency, Deborah is gone and the laundry is done. Angel. I throw enough tiny shirts and blankets into a suitcase to last a month, grab the car seat, and head out. On my way, I stop at the Dydee Diaper Service in Pasadena, conveniently located two blocks from the hospital. Because we don't want a landfill named after us, we're going with reusable *cloth* diapers. They give me a starter kit: three hampers, fifteen plastic diaper covers, and one hundred eighty cloth diapers.

The hospital needs us to name our babies. They like it when newborns leave the hospital with names. It completes the paperwork. But we don't have names yet. We were working on a short list before the triplets were born, but now we want to get to know them a little bit before we name them. We've read that a lot of parents of triplets name their kids in alphabetical order—Able, Baker, and Charlie—or with the same first initial—Mark, Miles, and Michael. We're *not* doing that. We're not sure what we're doing, but it's bringing back a childhood memory.

When I was in high school and finally old enough to drive, I needed to take a copy of my birth certificate to the Department of Motor Vehicles (DMV). My mom dug into the wonderful old antique desk in which she kept all her important papers and handed me a yellowed envelope containing my birth certificate from Hidalgo County, Texas. As I examined it with great curiosity, I noticed the name on my birth certificate was "Casady Boy #5."

"Oh, imagine that," my mom confessed. "I guess we never got around to letting the County Recorder know the name we picked for you."

Uh, yeah. This was going to be a problem at the DMV. I had to collect an assortment of documents—report cards, medical records, junior high school diploma—to prove to the county recorder in Texas that my given name is Cort Boon Casady. Yes, I was a little traumatized by this, but now, many decades later, with three children of my own, I can relate.

Barb has been in the hospital for four days, including the day she delivered the boys. The hospital is saying we can leave without naming the boys, so long as we promise to let them know their names soon. Of course, we will. And our three boys will leave Huntington Hospital officially known as "Casady Baby A," "Casady Baby B," and "Casady Baby C."

By about 6:30 p.m., Barb's been discharged, and we're checking out with Baby B, leaving Babies A and C behind in the NIC Unit—a tough moment. It feels very strange to leave two of our babies behind. We pack Baby B into the car seat and pull out. He promptly begins to cry, and we learn lesson number one in the parenting business: the sound of a baby crying is like a smoke alarm. It's designed to be heard, and you're meant to do something about it. Barb wants to pull over and do something. The thing is, I figure that once you put the baby in the car seat and start driving, you can't take him out to comfort him. Kind of defeats the purpose of the car seat.

So I say, "Don't worry; he'll be fine. We're on our way." I figure this is what dads do, right? Or is it? The kid's screaming as we pull onto the freeway. This is going to be the longest thirty minutes of our lives. I put on a classical music station and suddenly, miraculously, the motion of the car, the music, whatever—Baby B stops crying. It's then that we learn lesson number two: the only thing more alarming than a baby crying is when he suddenly stops! Barb checks to make sure the baby is alive, and we keep going. The drive home is quiet, peaceful, wonderful. We're parents!

Before we go up the hill, we stop at Thrifty Drug Store to get pain medication for Barb. She and the baby wait in the car, awash in classical music. All good.

### *January 11, 1995 – Baby Nurse Number One*

About an hour after we get home, Gladys Flowers, the baby nurse, arrives. We're relieved. She's a kindly Black woman in her early sixties from Belize. Gladys has cared for triplets before. She instills confidence. The nursery still isn't set up, but we will get through the night.

Mother, father, Baby B, and Gladys awaken to a new day and unexpected news. Gladys says her husband is ill and she must leave. Thus begins the Day from Hell. It's a three-ring circus. Gladys needs a ride, but I can't leave Barb, and she can't leave the baby. So Gladys calls a nephew or cousin, and I try to give him directions. He sounds drunk, definitely sleepy, maybe sleeping off a bender, I don't know, but giving him directions is not easy. Barb is in bed calling other baby nurses. She has endured a dangerous, high-risk pregnancy during which she became the size of Montana. She suffered sudden premature labor and emergency C-section surgery, gave up her three babies to the harsh lights of an operating room and a group of strangers, had the babies taken from her to separate nurseries in the hospital, and was allowed to go home with only one; now, she's on the phone calling baby nurses to replace the one we're losing. Super mom, super wife.

That night, Donna Halloran arrives. She's a shift nurse. She's covering from 10:00 p.m. to 7:00 a.m.—the midnight and 4:00 a.m. feedings. She's a godsend.

### *Friday, January 13, 1995 – Baby Nurse Number Two*

The three-ring circus continues. Doorbell rings. It's Adeline Bannister, the new baby nurse who will replace Donna, the fill-in person. Adeline is Black, wearing a white nurse's outfit and more jewelry than Mr. T. (Look it up: mid-1980s TV series called *The A-Team*.) Rings in her ears. Rings on her fingers. Fancy watch. Gold necklace with her name, "Adeline," on it, which is helpful so we don't call her "Gladys" or "Donna" through the fog of war. She steps in and says, "Boy, it was hard to find this place. You want me? 'Cause if you don't, I don't want to let my ride go."

"We want you!"

*Sunday, January 15, 1995 - Baby Nurse Number Three*

Two days later, I pick up Baby A from the neonatal intensive care unit. He's the one the doctors thought had inhaled some blood during birth. Turns out he didn't, but he has had some difficulty maintaining his body temperature. We're advised to keep one of the knit hats I bought at Toys "R" Us on him at all times. I put him in a car seat and drive him home to be reunited with his mother and his brother in a nursery which now has three cribs. He's all good.

After three days, Adeline wants to quit. She has enormous hands, the babies are small, and she tells me she's afraid she might hurt them. The fact that she's afraid makes us afraid. We agree she should go. The new baby nurse is Gertrude ("Gertie"). She's the daughter of Louella, who had been highly recommended but isn't available. Gertie is amazing. She'll be with us for the next five days and nights.

Baby C is still in the NICU. He's healthy, but he needs to gain weight. When he's over four pounds, they'll let him come home. Barbara's got her hands and her blouse full, nursing the two babies who are home and pumping breast milk for Baby C. I collect the breast milk from the freezer and drive it to the hospital every day. The nurses are thrilled to see me because they know I'm the "Mother's Milk Man." And I'm thrilled to see Baby C. He's in an incubator with a device attached to his foot to monitor his vital signs. He doesn't look comfortable, but he's thriving and gaining weight.

To enter the NICU, I have to "scrub in," put on a blue gown, hat, and mask, wash my hands and arms with disinfectant like they do before surgery on *Grey's Anatomy*, then put on gloves. I love seeing little Baby C and imparting some love and comfort with mother's milk and a father's touch. I really want to take him home.

## *January 23, 1995 – A Full House*

Two weeks after the triplets were born, I get to bring Baby C home. One of the nurses walks with us to the car. She helps me put him in a car seat and, after he's all buckled up, she says: "Mr. Casady, the triplets are on a schedule for feeding and changing, and we strongly recommend you keep them on this schedule."

I say, "Sure, thanks, will do." The nurse takes me by the shoulders, looks me squarely in the eye, and says sternly, "I'm not kidding, Mr. Casady. You need to keep them on a schedule, or you'll be in serious trouble."

"Okay, okay. We will."

## *January 24, 1995*

The triplets are all at home. The nursery is set up. The house is humming with life. The handwriting on Marta came back "recommended," so she's living in a room downstairs. Marta's very sweet and a hard worker. And there's a lot of work. We're constantly mixing formula, making meals, changing diapers, washing dishes, changing diapers, mixing more formula, doing laundry. Did I mention changing diapers? I think we're doing thirty-six diapers a day (twelve each), or at least it smells that way. Do the math: that's roughly eleven hundred diapers a month.

The diaper service brings us about three hundred diapers per week. Once a week, they pick up the dirty diapers, which they don't want us to empty or rinse out. We put them in three hampers with lids that fit very tightly, which is key, or we would have to move out of our house. The service comes and collects "the dirties" from the hampers, takes them to Pasadena, washes and sterilizes them, and returns our clean diapers the next week. So, once a week, this wonderful man pulls up in the Dydee Diaper truck, takes the bags of dirty diapers from the three bins, and drives away—usually, I notice, while smoking an enormous cigar. Bless his heart.

The show called "Three of Everything" is in full production. The baby nurses have trained us in the care and feeding of newborns. Marta's working hard. Three cribs, three diaper hampers, three sets of baby bottles, three highchairs, three bouncy chairs, three playpens, three car seats. We don't have a triplet stroller, because we can't imagine anyone wanting to go out alone with all three babies, so we have two strollers, a single and a double.

It's 8:30 p.m. The babies are in their cribs. The kitchen is quiet. Marta's in her bed. Barbara's getting ready for bed. I'm taking the trash out. I'm standing in front of our house looking back at it. The lights are on. The house is full of babies and full of life. And I'm having the most sobering thought of my life: I'm responsible for this family.

A few days later. Awkward New Dad Moment: After all the babies are home, I go out and buy a baby monitor and set it up. After a couple of nights, I say to Barb, "Honey, I'm confused. Why do the babies need to hear everything *we're* doing?"

### The Name Game

Now that we've gotten to know the boys, we're ready to name them. Instead of calling them Baby A, B, and C, they are Braden Chandler Casady, Carter Boon Casady, and Jackson Mercer Casady. The hospital is thrilled. Official birth certificates are on their way. In choosing the middle names, we've consciously included the maiden names of the women in both of our families: Chandler is Barbara's mother's maiden name; Boon is my mother's maiden name; Mercer is Barbara's maiden name.

The triplets are on a schedule. No kidding. Their little lives are scheduled like the Swiss railroad. Feeding, followed by burping, diaper change, nap, playtime, feeding, bath, reading, music, and so on. And they're so in tune with their schedule that the three of them go off like an alarm clock every four hours when it's time to eat.

You think I'm kidding? I found this in a file:

|  |  |
|---|---|
| 7:30 a.m. | Prepare protein drink for Barbara (Marta) |
| 7:45 a.m. | Protein drink upstairs |
| 8:00 a.m. | Feed Babies (breast feed first, then bottles) (Barb & Marta) |
| 9:00 a.m. | Change & Bathe Babies, Pump Breast Milk (Barbara), Prepare Breakfast (Marta) |
| 9:00 a.m. to Noon | Babies' playtime |
| 10:00 a.m. | Eat Breakfast (Barb, Cort, Marta) |
| 10:30 a.m. to 12 Noon | Open (Showers, phone calls, clean up, etc.) |
| 12:00 p.m. | Feed & Change Babies (Barb & Marta) |
| 1:00 p.m. | Pump Breast Milk (Barbara) |
| 1:00 p.m. to 2:30 p.m. | Babies' Naptime |
| 1:30 p.m. | Prepare & Eat Lunch |
| 2:30 p.m. to 4:00 p.m. | Open (Work, shop, run errands, etc.) |
| 4:00 p.m. | Feed & Change Babies (Barb & Marta) |
| 5:00 p.m. | Pump Breast Milk (Barbara) |

| | |
|---|---|
| 5:00 p.m. to 7:00 p.m. | Babies' Playtime |
| 7:00 p.m. | Dinner (Barb, Cort, Marta) |
| 8:00 p.m. | Feed & Change Babies, Babies' Bedtime |
| 9:00 p.m. | Pump Breast Milk (Barb) |
| 9:30 p.m. | All Sleep |
| 12:00 a.m. | Feed & Change Babies |
| 1:00 a.m. | All Sleep |
| 4:00 a.m. | Feed & Change Babies |
| 5:00 a.m. | All Sleep |
| 7:30 a.m. | Prepare protein drink for Barbara (Marta) |
| 7:45 a.m. | Protein drink upstairs |
| 8:00 a.m. | Feed Babies (breast feed first, then bottles) (Barb & Marta) |
| 9:00 a.m. | Change & Bathe Babies |
| 9:30 a.m. | Pump Breast Milk (Barbara) Prepare Breakfast (Marta) |
| 10:00 a.m. | Eat Breakfast |

As preemies, the boys' immune systems are still vulnerable, so for the first six weeks, everyone who comes in the house is asked to wash their hands thoroughly. One morning, some friends come over for a visit after the 8:00 a.m. feeding, burping, and changing. They wash their hands, and we sit around the dining room table. Next thing we know, four hours have gone by. We know it's noon because the three babies start crying at exactly twelve o'clock. Barb rushes upstairs to the nursery. Marta and I are warming supplemental bottles of formula. A few minutes later, I'm walking into the nursery with the bottles, and all is quiet. No crying. I'm wondering, *How is this possible?* Barbara's on the bed with one boy on each breast and her knuckle in the mouth of the third one. And I get it: I can't do that.

*February 5, 1995*

Sunday morning. Marta's day off. I'm about to drive her to the bus stop. As Marta gets in the car, she turns to Barbara and says sweetly, "Bye, Missus. Don't work too hard."

Monday morning after the 8:00 a.m. feeding, while I'm keeping an eye on the babies, Barbara goes to pick up Marta. Marta's not there. Barbara waits. Marta doesn't show. Back at the house, Barbara calls Marta and Marta's daughter. No answer.

Two days go by. Still no Marta. Finally, Barb reaches the daughter who tells her Marta went to the hospital with some kind of "scare." She had heart palpitations.

Marta calls a few days later and asks us to pick her up at a certain time. Again, she doesn't show. We're up the proverbial creek without a paddle, and we have no choice but to carry on.

The babies' four-hour feeding schedule is unrelenting. Barb's nursing, and we're supplementing with formula. And we don't actually get four hours between feedings because, even with two people, it takes an hour and a half to feed, burp and change all three then clean up afterwards and get ready for the next feeding. By the time we finish the 4:00 p.m. feeding, for example, it's almost 6:00 p.m., which leaves about an hour and forty-five minutes to two hours until the next feeding. This goes on around the clock, 24-7 . . . 8:00 a.m., noon, 4:00 p.m., 8:00 p.m., midnight, 4:00 a.m., 8:00 a.m.

We're fried. We're so tired, we're telling government secrets we don't even know. And we're wandering around asking each other, "Where's Marta?"

We have to hire another nanny, but there's hardly any time to interview anyone. After the 8:00 a.m. feeding, we have a window from about 10:00 a.m. until 11:30 a.m. and another window from about 2:00 p.m. until about 3:30. Our time is so limited that if a candidate is a "no-show," it's depressing. A friend recommends we hire a registered nurse (RN) to cover the graveyard shift so we can sleep. And graveyard seems like a possible destination if we don't get help soon.

A few nights later, we're waiting for the nurse to show up. She's an RN who has been caring for terminally ill cancer patients. She's excited to see our three little babies who are so full of life. We agree to pay her one hundred dollars so we can go to bed at 10:00 p.m. and sleep through the midnight and 4:00 a.m. feedings. She's got this, and off to slumber we go.

About three o'clock in the morning, I wake up to loud popping and crackling sounds. Barbara's sound asleep. The RN and the babies are asleep in the nursery. Out the back window, I can see a bright red glow up the hill behind us. In front of our house, fire trucks are lined up on the street as far as I can see in both directions, lights flashing. Looking out the rear window again, I see that a house up the hill from ours is on fire.

By now, Barbara's awake and not happy about it, asking what's going on. She's exhausted and doesn't want to get up. Remember, we're *paying for sleep*. "Honey, I think the house behind us is on fire."

She rolls over and says, "Is our house on fire?"

I say, "No."

She says, "Wake me up when our house is on fire." And goes right back to sleep!

The next morning, we learn that the owner of the house up the hill had stored some ammunition in the garage. The popping sound was bullets exploding. So the firefighters were forced to back off and let the house burn down, while making sure the fire didn't spread to other houses.

### *Casady for Mayor*

Without a nanny or a nurse on board, we're both up for the midnight and 4:00 a.m. feedings. Sitting in the nursery in the wee hours, we have time to think. Sometimes, we talk about Barb's mom, Francie, gone too soon and long ago. She would have loved these babies. Sometimes, we think about my mom, Virginia, and wish we had had our boys when she was still alive and we were younger. Sometimes, we fondly remember places we traveled together: France, Italy, Tahiti, Hawaii, Tortola in the British Virgin Islands.

This morning at 4:00 a.m. in the nursery, I'm thinking about my dad and how, at the age of seventy-one, he got talked into running for mayor of San Diego against a two-term incumbent Republican named Pete Wilson. It's 1979. My father has covered politics his whole life, but he's not a politician. He's a retired newspaper man and a recovering antiwar activist who has spent several years traveling the world with my mother. But he's passionate about making sure we have a government of the people, by the people, and for the people. Some folks asked him to run for mayor. He knows he's a "sacrificial lamb"—meaning he knows he won't win—but he's running anyway, and I respect that. I'm working in Hollywood as a TV staff writer. I volunteer to go to San Diego for a few weeks to produce Pop's TV spots, and my brother, Kent, volunteers to pay for them.

I'm pretty sure my dad has no idea what I do for a living or, if he does, he doesn't think it's a "real" job. One morning, after I've been toiling for a week or so in the dining room of our "campaign headquarters," trying to come up with ideas for TV commercials, Pop stops by the bathroom while I'm shaving. He stands in the doorway and says, "I've been thinking. I don't think we should be doing TV spots. I don't want to be sold like soap," he says. "Besides, TV's just a piece of furniture. We're newspaper people, not TV people." With that, he turns and walks away. I follow him, feeling ambushed and flabbergasted at the same time.

"Pop," I call out, "remember the Kennedy-Nixon debates in 1960?" I know he does because, even though we didn't own a TV when I was growing up, Pop rented one every four years during the presidential campaigns. "Kennedy won the election because of television. Television is the most important tool in politics. Every campaign since has used television. You may think TV's just piece of furniture," I continue, "but millions of people gather around that piece of furniture and watch things like the Super Bowl and the Academy Awards. You need TV ads." He doesn't want to hear it.

"And let me tell you something you don't know about television," I continue brashly.

Pop stops, meets my gaze, and says sternly, "You can't tell me *anything* I don't know." And walks away.

I'm hurt. I get dressed and drive around San Diego for a couple of hours, trying to decide whether to stay or leave the campaign and go back to LA. When I finally come back to the house, Pop's waiting for me.

"My campaign manager just quit," he says solemnly. "He's going to Hawaii on vacation. I need you to help run my campaign."

So I stay.

Pop's passionate about social and economic justice. Early in the campaign at a rally in Balboa Park, someone asks him, "Are you for rent control?" Typically, rent control is a hot-button issue in a mayoral campaign. Renters love it; apartment owners hate it; voters are divided about it. I wonder what he's going to say.

"I'm for *greed control*," he intones, to the delight of the crowd.

Brilliant answer. Who isn't for greed control? "Greed" is defined as "a selfish, excessive, often uncontrolled desire for more of something (such as money) than is needed." Greed is one of those things we're never going to get rid of but, in a fair and just society, it's one of those things we need to temper with intelligent rules and regulations. Unfortunately, as we've come to find out over the past four decades, a lot of American corporations and lawmakers don't believe in greed control and, in countless ways, ordinary Americans are paying the price.

After days in the dining room at a typewriter—that's right, before computers—I finally come up with copy for two ads that I think will work. Both are designed to be controversial in the hope that they will attract more *free media* attention than we can afford to buy for them on television. One of the ads features an empty policeman's uniform turning dramatically in a shaft of light as the announcer intones, "Thousands of police officers have left San Diego because Pete Wilson is tough on cops. Si Casady will be tough on *crime*, not cops." In the other ad, a big yellow bulldozer with a Pete Wilson button on the blade comes at the camera, clearing brush and pushing dirt out of the way as the announcer warns: "Pete Wilson has been selling city-owned land to his campaign contributors for half price. He's turning San Diego into another Los Angeles." Pop steps in front of the bulldozer, it stops, and he says: "I'm Si Casady, and I'll stop this reckless growth." The statements are true. My father has already made the allegation about the mayor selling city-owned land in a story in the *San Diego Union-Tribune*. The newspaper article attracted zero attention.

We get lucky. One morning, a reporter from the *Los Angeles Times* calls our "headquarters." She's heard that the candidate's sons are producing and paying for his TV ads, and I confirm what she's heard. My brother, Kent, has offered to pay for the ads; I've offered to produce them. When she asks what the ads will say, I read her the actual scripts. She prints the content of both spots verbatim in the San Diego edition of the *LA Times*. Wilson goes nuts. The allegations are headline news, especially the one about the mayor selling city-owned land to his contributors. Wilson threatens to sue my father for libel and demands that the local TV stations refuse to air the spots. This doesn't work. Wilson has forgotten that my father is a newspaper man who knows something about libel laws. Pop says when Wilson's attorneys weigh in, Wilson will learn he hasn't been libeled.

It doesn't hurt that, in 1979, TV stations are still guided by Federal Communications Commission (FCC) rules and something called the Fairness Doctrine. Introduced in 1949, the Fairness Doctrine requires the holders of broadcast licenses to present controversial issues of public importance and to do so in a manner that is, in the commission's view, honest, equitable, and balanced. If they don't comply, their licenses can be pulled. The stations decide that our TV spots are "a bona fide expression by a candidate for public office" and, therefore, cannot be censored. Before our bulldozer ad airs in any of the time slots we've purchased for it, the spot is being shown in its entirety on the 6:00, 10:00, and 11:00 p.m. newscasts on every TV station in San Diego. Not just free exposure but free exposure *during the news* where you can't buy time for political ads. Our modest little television campaign is working even better than we thought it would.

Pop didn't win the election, but our TV campaign helped him earn 35 percent of the vote which, the pundits thought, was extraordinary in an underfunded race against an eight-year incumbent. During the campaign, Pop told audiences that "Pete Wilson wants to be anything but mayor of San Diego." He was right. After serving as a state assemblyman for two years and three terms as mayor of San Diego, Wilson went on to become a two-term US senator (1983-1991) then quit the Senate to run for governor, won twice (1991 and 1995), and, finally, ran unsuccessfully for president.

When the campaign was over, Pop thanked me for producing the TV spots and acknowledged how important they had been. He told me he thought I was a pretty good writer and producer and that he finally understood what I did for a living. As the youngest in the family, I never felt I was heard, least of all by my father. Clearly, this time, and maybe for the first time, Pop heard me. It was a sweet moment that profoundly transformed our relationship and remains one of my fondest memories of him to this day.

*February 21, 1995*

The babies are six weeks old. We're taking them to the pediatrician for their first checkup. Three babies, three car seats across the back seat of the Explorer, two parents. Without a nanny, we're one parent shy of a perfect family. I lug two car seats with two babies; Barb lugs the other one, and in we go to Dr. Fred Friedman's office.

We unpack the babies one at a time and present them to the obviously amused doctor. Our brains are fried, but we do comprehend one thing: thank goodness, they're all healthy, whole, and developing normally. Dr. Friedman wants to know whether we've been keeping track of how much they're eating. Is he kidding? We can hardly put one foot in front of the other without stumbling. In the melee of feeding three hungry babies every four hours, including in the middle of the night when they're awake and we aren't, no, we have not been keeping track of how much they're eating. But we say we'll try.

Dr. Friedman sends us on our way with these words of wisdom, spoken in his best consoling-new-parents voice: "You can get through this with a sense of humor and a well-stocked bar."

He's right. We stop at the Liquor Locker on the way home. And for the first time, I tell the boys, "I drink because you cry."

Meanwhile, naming the boys does help us keep track of how much they're eating. The challenge has been, when you're feeding one boy from a bottle and you set the bottle down to feed another boy, how do you remember later whose bottle that was? Especially at four in the morning? I deploy a piece of shirt-cardboard to make a placemat with three circles on it: one marked "C," one marked "B," and one marked "J." When we finish feeding Jackson, we place his bottle on the circle with the "J." At the end of the feeding frenzy, we can accurately record how much formula Jackson consumed. As for breast milk, Dr. Friedman suggests that Barbara keep track of how long she breastfeeds each baby. We create charts and record the times and amounts for each feeding for each baby, each day. Over the next six months, the charts fill a three-inch-thick three-ring binder. Dr. Friedman never, ever mentions the subject again or asks to see our fastidious records. No worries. We can submit them with their college applications.

*Nanny Search*

Marta was with us for nearly three weeks before she vanished. We struggled for three weeks with intermittent night shift help. Then, several weeks after she disappeared, Marta telephones us out of the blue. "Hi, Missus, how are you?" She offers no explanation for where she's been but says she would like to come back to work. We're worried about her health. Barbara tells her, "No thanks, we're good."

We're not good. We're desperate for a nanny. Our house is starting to feel like the *Titanic*. Without an orchestra. We're on our own, and we're going down. We're not looking for help because we're rich or lazy or don't want to take care of our kids. We *need* help because we've got three babies and no grandparents. We're exhausted; we're outnumbered; and we're both trying to work. Childcare for three babies in daycare is expensive. We priced it. And parents know, if you pick your kid up late from daycare, times three, they really sock it to you.

We receive an application from the Happy Day Domestic Agency and interview an experienced nurse/nanny named Ann Maria Semakula for the day shift. Ann Maria lives in Palmdale with her sister, about an hour and half from Encino. Her lilting accent makes us think she has immigrated from Uganda, but we're not sure. She has kids of her own. The handwriting examiner recommends her; she's willing to work the day shift and live in during the week. We hire her and quickly discover that Ann Maria is kind, attentive, thorough, loves fruit juice, and takes good care of the boys. Now, if we could only find someone to cover the night shift.

I think our prayers have been answered when a very attractive brunette shows up for an interview. Her resume indicates that she's currently the reigning Miss Detroit. She's an aspiring actress who has performed in all the Gilbert and Sullivan musicals. Impressive. She comes from a large family, has extensive babysitting experience, and wants to work with a family at night so her days will be free to audition for acting jobs. Oh, and her mother is a neonatal nurse. Perfect. She's sweet, experienced, family-oriented, and happens to be gorgeous. Barbara meets her and, the minute the young woman is gone, has two words: "No way."

"In the middle of the night, when I'm in a baggy pajamas with bed-hair, I'm not having a woman in full theatrical makeup with a body like that in the nursery."

I get it. We're hiring a hunchback. Barb's not about to have me pull "a Piscopo" which is named after one-time *Saturday Night Live* performer Joe Piscopo. Joe ran off with the babysitter. She was gorgeous. She was eighteen. And, no surprise, it blew up his marriage. Which is why running off with the babysitter is called "a Piscopo." To be clear, it's *not* "a Schwarzenegger." "A Schwarzenegger" is where you poke the maid (or nanny), but nobody finds out. "A *Full* Schwarzenegger" is where you get the maid pregnant, she has the baby, and you go through a humiliating and costly divorce.

A few days later, the handwriting examiner calls. She's been looking over the nanny applications again and thinks one of the candidates could be a good fit for the night shift. The applicant doesn't speak much English, she says, but her temperament and character are excellent. She thinks we might have met her before, but we're in such a haze, who knows? We schedule an interview.

While the boys are napping, the doorbell rings and in walks Genoveva Martinez Suarez. She's friendly, has a sparkle in her eyes and reassuring energy, and she's short. No shaming here, but she's so short that I take

Barb aside and ask, "How's this going to work? This woman has *no lap*. Her legs are so short that when she sits down, there's hardly any place to rest a baby. She's going to need a lap, isn't she?" Barb looks at me and says what any intelligent mother in search of a nanny would say: "Shut up."

Genoveva likes to be called "Geno" (pronounced "*Heh-no*") and as warned, her English is limited. We realize we did meet her before but didn't hire her because of the language barrier. We speak some Spanish, so we're doing our illiterate best to give her another shot.

We take Geno upstairs to the nursery to meet the babies then into the bathroom for a round of diaper changing. Geno tells us she has raised two sons, but it's clear she hasn't changed diapers in a while. It's clear because I, as one of the two world-class, Olympic-level Diapering Masters in the house, must step in to make a few corrections. Geno's confident, though, and a quick study. She nails number two and number three as we explain the job. She'll come each night around seven and help with the eight o'clock feeding and changing. She'll sleep in the nursery with the babies and do the midnight and 4:00 a.m. feedings by herself. It's a big job, but she seems up to it. Geno's a naturalized citizen and currently working in a sewing shop downtown. For similar pay, this will be way better work.

The handwriting examiner speaks Spanish fluently, so we call her back and ask her to talk to Geno. After they speak, the examiner tells us that Geno wants the job, but she's not sure if she can do it. If we give her a trial week, she'll let us know at the end of the week. We're impressed.

The trial week goes smoothly. The babies are getting fed and changed at midnight and 4:00 a.m. We're sleeping through the night. When we come into the nursery in the morning, Geno is asleep in her bed and the babies are in their cribs, swaddled snugly in their blankets, tipped at the perfect angle with their heads slightly elevated, looking very content. At 7:00 a.m. when she goes home, Geno seems no worse for the wear. Best of all, at week's end, she tells us she can do the job. Hallelujah!

*March 4, 1995*

Michael Douglas is being honored by the Santa Barbara International Film Festival (SBIFF) with its "Modern Master Award," and we're invited. Santa Barbara is a two-hour drive from our home in Encino. We really want to go. For one precious adult night out. Do we dare? We feel confident about leaving the triplets for twenty-four hours in the care of Ann Maria and Geno. The boys' Uncle Derek and Aunt Nancy are on alert, and Barbara's father, Dr. Mercer, is about an hour away.

The event is at the picturesque old Arlington Theatre. The ceremony is followed by a VIP dinner at a local restaurant. At dinner, we're seated across from Michael and Diandra, his wife at the time. At one point, Barb hands Michael a snapshot of the Casady Triplets. His eyes light up.

"Oh wow!" he exclaims and shows Diandra the photo. "Look," he says joyfully, "the Casadys have triplets!" Diandra shoots Michael a frosty look, and we get the impression things are strained between them. Michael's expression fades as he hands the snapshot back to us with a warm, "Congratulations."

Our hotel room is near the beach, but I can't hear the ocean. As I drift off to sleep, all I hear is the hissing and sucking sound of dear Barbara pumping breast milk for her boys. All good.

*March 27, 1995*

My dad, Simon Casady, "Pop," died today, three months after our sons were born. Before he passed, he met the babies and had a chance to hold each one in his arms. Pop loved babies, and his eyes lit up when he held our three.

*April 22, 1995*

My birthday, which I share with Earth Day. Barbara's working on her design projects. I'm writing infomercials. I've never written infomercials before or since, but this is great. I've taken one meeting outside of the house. Otherwise, I write the scripts, fax them to the producer, get notes, make revisions, and fax them back. The work is a godsend. I'm at home, earning good money, with plenty of time to bond with our boys. I will always be grateful to producer Pat Finn for giving me this work and for allowing me to do it while spending precious time at home with my new family.

*May 13, 1995*

The triplets are just over four months old. We're invited to attend a rehearsal brunch for my niece, Keri, who's getting married on Sunday to Ken Roberts. Our practice is to always have two caregivers in the house if we're going out, so if anything happens to one of the boys, there'll be someone to tend to the other two. Since we're going to a daytime event and we only have Ann Maria here during the day (Geno will come at 7:00 p.m.), Barbara's father, a retired doctor, is going to be Ann Maria's backup until Geno arrives. Barb and I are dressed and ready to go. Dr. Mercer has just arrived. Ann Maria is at the kitchen sink washing a glass Pyrex measuring cup.

We hear breaking glass. Ann Maria shrieks. We rush to see what's happened. The glass slipped out of her hands and broke just as she reached to catch it. She has a big gash in her hand. There's blood everywhere.

Dr. Mercer takes charge immediately. He staunches the bleeding, reassures Ann Maria that she's going to be okay, and offers to run to the drugstore for some butterfly bandages to close the wound. As he leaves, we realize there's another reason to have *two* caregivers. We always thought the reason to have backup was if something happens to one of the boys. We never imagined a scenario in which something happens to the caregiver. Fortunately, our backup is Marshall M. Mercer, MD. Thank you, doctor!

Barbara stays behind with her father and Ann Maria, who is out of commission. I head out alone to the rehearsal brunch for Keri and Kenny, grateful that an unexpected mishap didn't turn into a greater emergency.

*May 15, 1995*

Ann Maria is leaving us. Her hand is healing and, although her wound didn't require stitches, it has limited her activity. After being seen by a physician in Lancaster, she'll receive hand therapy for two weeks at a clinic in Beverly Hills. Taking her place during the day will be Hilda Rios. We are blessed to have her.

*July 4, 1995*

Time for the Fourth of July Mercer Family Reunion. Braden, Carter, and Jackson are six months old. This time, Barbara's family is gathering at her Uncle Jim's house in Irvine, about an hour and a half drive south. At this point, moving our family of five plus Genoveva anywhere is what we call in the movie business "a company move." Everything has to go with us. Our dear friend Raymond Jacobi is the general manager of the Four Seasons Hotel on Fashion Island in Newport Beach, which is only a short drive from Uncle Jim's. Raymond invites us to stay at the hotel—complimentary—so we don't have to drive down and drive back in one day or arrange for financing to pay the going rate at the Four Seasons. We're thrilled and grateful. We'll stay two nights.

Road trip!

Packing the Explorer makes for an alarming snapshot of our life. A playpen, two strollers, and several suitcases are strapped to the top of the car. Three car seats fill the second row. (It's a five-seater.) There are more suitcases in the back, including an enormous one filled with disposable diapers. Yeah, we're not taking the Dydee Diaper poopy pails.

Geno's sitting in the back, surrounded by suitcases and leaning against one of those sit-up-in-bed pillows to form a makeshift seat. Totally illegal. Totally embarrassing. When we pull into the luxurious Four Seasons Hotel, we look like something out of John Steinbeck's *The Grapes of Wrath*. I'm expecting one of the bellmen to yell, "Hey, look, the Joads are here!"

Instead, we're greeted by a tall gentleman in a three-piece suit and top hat who says, "Welcome to the Four Seasons, Mr. Casady." What? We find out later that the bell staff is alerted to the arrival of "VIP guests" or, in this case, a party with more than one stroller and a playpen on top of the car. We're astonished. We help Geno climb out, grateful that she can still walk; we haul the boys out in their car seats and stand for a moment, staring at our jam-packed car.

The bellman says politely, "Would you like everything to go up to the room, Mr. Casady?"

I look at Barb, Barb looks at Geno, Geno looks at me, and I say to the bellman, "Yes, please."

Our room is not just a room. It's the Governor's Suite. Entry foyer, powder room, living room, baby grand piano, dining area with a bar, two bedrooms, and an office with a fax machine. In one of the bedrooms, in addition to two double beds, there are three cribs, each adorned with a balloon, a stuffed bear, baby shampoo, lotion, and diapers. We are slack-jawed and overjoyed. Thank you, Ray!

The next morning. Geno's up. Barb's still asleep. I'm playing with the boys on the floor in the living room of our glorious suite. It's wonderful. Our lives are so full of *doing* for them—changing, feeding, loading, unloading, shopping, cooking, deploying toys, cleaning up toys—that sometimes it feels like we don't spend enough time just *being* with them. On this rare and glorious morning, I'm just hangin' with "the trips." And it hits me. We treat them equally, care for them as one. But what I'm seeing in them is how different they are. They are truly individuals.

Jackson is a happy guy who looks slightly worried at times, and he has an easy laugh. He sometimes cries preemptively, before anything happens. Braden is patient. When the other two are crying for their bottles at mealtime, Braden is content to wait quietly, confident he'll get fed. Carter is curious and eager to crawl around checking things out.

I make up a little song and sing to them softly as we play:

WE ARE THREE INDIVIDUALS
ONE-TWO-THREE, INDIVIDUALS
WE ARE THREE INDIVIDUALS
ONE-TWO-THREE

At the Mercer Family Reunion, we're received like royalty and a circus oddity. We set up the playpen and deploy various other pieces of equipment in a back bedroom—our temporary nursery. Our relatives are amazed. Barb's Uncle Bob offers each boy a finger to grab. "They've got a good strong grip," he says. The women comment on how cute they are. We're grateful to be here. Truth is, we're grateful to be anywhere.

As a father, I'm growing and learning every day. I'm discovering things about babies and nursing moms. For example, whenever a woman who's nursing hears a baby cry, her milk "lets down," and she starts to ooze breast milk. With three crying babies, Barbara's nipples are like the Tilt-A-Whirl at a carnival. If we go somewhere by ourselves to get a little respite from our babies, inevitably someone else's baby cries in the vicinity and Barb's nipples say: "Come and get it!"

Our trip to Newport makes us realize how fortunate we are to have Genoveva. We're free to visit with Barb's relatives and enjoy the festivities, knowing Geno will tend to the boys. At home, Hilda, a delightful Latina woman, has replaced Ann Maria during the day. Once the boys start sleeping through the night, Geno will join Hilda for the day shift. Later, when Hilda leaves, she'll be replaced full-time time by Geno's wonderful and tireless friend Rosa Correa and, from time to time, Rosa's daughter, Dulce. The extra hands, extra care, and extra love are deeply appreciated.

## *The Christmas Card*

We're starting a family tradition: an annual Christmas card. The plan is to take a great picture of the boys each year and mail out cards to friends and family so they can watch the boys grow up and keep up with their exploits. It's also a way for us to mark another year of survival.

October 1995. Curtis Dahl, the gifted photographer who married my one-time assistant, Bren Bennington, agrees to take our pictures at his studio. But the boys are nine months old and very squirmy. Keeping them in the shot is like herding cats, except cats would be easier. Barb is wrangling them, trying to hold the three tightly on her lap. Curtis, who is nothing if not patient, is clicking away like mad. But this is before digital photography; he's shooting film and unable to see what he's got as we go. He and we won't see anything until the film is developed and printed! At the end of the session, Curtis looks drained and says, "I'm not sure I got anything you can use."

A few days later, Curtis surprises us with a great photo we can use for our first Christmas card. The tradition is born. Across the years, Curtis will train the triplets to sit still, compose themselves, and take direction, and with his keen eye and gift for composition, he will shoot dozens of remarkable photos of our family growing up. (Our card becomes so popular that friends tell us they keep them on their refrigerators all year long, until they get the new one, and some say they're saving them all.)

Now that the boys are eating solid food and the midnight and 4:00 a.m. feedings are a thing of the past, we're recovering, and our mission is to have the boys sleep through the night from 7:00 p.m. to 7:00 a.m. To accomplish this, we decide to give the world-famous Ferber Method a try. When one child wakes up in the night crying, the book—the Method—instructs you to make sure the child is okay, comfort them, make sure they're warm enough, rub their back, but don't pick them up. Leave the room for a few minutes, even if they're still crying. If the child is still crying after a couple of minutes, you go back in, comfort them, then leave again for a few more minutes. The promise of the book is that, after a week or two, the child will learn to put himself back to sleep.

What about three? Ferber doesn't say. In our experience, the boy who wakes up crying wakes up one of his brothers, and together, they wake up the third. Pretty soon it sounds like the Mormon Tabernacle Choir is crying. Nonetheless, we're going to treat the three as one: go in every few minutes when they're crying to make sure they're okay and have their blankets, rub their backs, and then leave them crying for a few minutes, if need be, before going back in to comfort them and so forth.

On night number three, we're following the drill. When they're crying, we sit on our bed waiting, hoping. It's torture. Nobody wants to hear their child crying. But then, after a few trips in and out of their room to comfort them, they all stop crying. We peek in, and all three boys have put themselves back to sleep. It works! And it feels like we just got a raise.

*Chapter 4*

# DIVING IN

> *One thing I learned from watching chimpanzees with their infants is that having children should be fun.*
> —JANE GOODALL, ENGLISH PRIMATOLOGIST

Our first year with triplets nearly killed us.

We were overwhelmed. Our live-in nanny, Marta, left us. We were sleep-deprived. We had trouble finding help. Then, by the grace of the universe, we found Ann Maria, Genoveva, and Hilda.

And finally, the boys are turning *one*.

As our babies become toddlers (technically ages one to three), we're still in the tunnel, but we can see light.

### January 7, 1996 – First Birthday

A child's first birthday is a Big Thing, a milestone. But let's be honest, it's an event that parents will never forget and children will never remember. As far as we can tell, first birthdays are for parents.

To celebrate the boys' first birthday, we invite all the parents we've met recently—four couples with triplets, one with twins, and one with a "singleton." (That's what parents of multiples call one child—a *singleton*.) So there are six sets of parents and fifteen kids at the party. It's a blast.

Lots of kids, food, cake, and some alcohol for the adults. At one point, I ask my friend Jim Novack, the father of the singleton, "So, with only one child, what do you do with all your spare time?" Couldn't resist.

*January 12, 1996 – Year Two Begins*

While writing this book, I discover various notes and journals poking up through our belongings like bones in an archeological dig. One surprising treasure is a three-ring binder in which Barbara recorded the boys' activities virtually every day for nine months during their *second* year, from January 1996 through September 1996. Having survived Year One, she found the time and energy to document that our life with three toddlers and two nannies is way easier than managing three babies by ourselves.

Barbara's notes mostly chronicle the course of each day as our one-year-olds follow their new schedule:

WINTER SCHEDULE 1/12/96
  7:00 a.m. – Good morning! Greet the boys. Change diapers.
  7:15 a.m. – Bottles of formula/milk
  7:30 a.m. – Play
  8:15 a.m. – Breakfast – Cereal, fruit, eggs, toast, etc.
  8:45 a.m. – Play
  9:30 a.m. – Morning nap in cribs
  11:00 a.m. – Play
  11:30 a.m. – Morning stroll (2 strollers) up the hill in the neighborhood
  12:00 p.m. – Bottles of formula/milk
  1:00 p.m. – Lunch – Vegetables, meats, and grains
  1:30 p.m. – Play or visit Tumble Time
  2:30 p.m. – Nap in cribs

3:30 p.m. – Wake up, have a snack: apple juice, graham crackers
4:00 p.m. – Afternoon stroll (2 strollers) in neighborhood
   or visit a park
5:00 p.m. – Bottles of formula/milk
6:00 p.m. – Dinner – Vegetables, meats and grains
6:30 p.m. – Play
7:15 p.m. – Baths
7:45 p.m. – Last bottles of formula/milk
8:00 p.m. – Bedtime – Reading, music, sleep – Goodnight angels!
   Sleep until 7 a.m. please

Note: Music, stories, Tumble Time, outside play dates, and park visits can be fit into any Play period.

*January 13, 1996*

What a difference a year makes.

Instead of feeling constantly overwhelmed by the care and feeding of three babies and the search for reliable help, we're able to enjoy our boys as burgeoning toddlers who can walk and, we can see, are becoming little *people*. Barbara's notes record joyful days, landmark moments, twice-daily strolls up the hill from our house, and a healthy number of runny noses, colds, fevers, and visits to Doctor Fred. Still, with Ann Maria, Geno, then Hilda coming each day and the guys sleeping through the night, our experience has been transformed.

For example, at one point, Barb records: "We love waking up with the boys. Seeing them first thing in the morning, no matter what our mood, puts a smile on our faces." Noted in many entries are the times when they do wake up: 6:00 a.m. (ouch) versus 6:30 (better) versus 7:30 (heavenly). Barb also notes that, when we come into the nursery, "They're hanging their arms over the edge of their cribs, babbling and yapping like neighbors chatting over a backyard fence." How great is that?

Before their first birthday month is over, we're at the Weiss's home for a second party, reuniting the group that hosted our shower, plus Dr. Batzofin and his wife, Diane. The food is great—Barbara made coq au vin—and there are lots of toasts. Kathy and Steve Coon and Marlo Bendau reprise the song from the shower. We're laughing, crying, and feeling enormously grateful.

*January 23, 1996*

This year, the annual National Association of Television Program Executives (NATPE) convention is in Las Vegas. I'm up before the boys and flying over for the day to schmooze and network with colleagues. My new business card for the occasion is a fold-over type with a picture of the triplets on the front. Inside, it reads: "Cort Casady, Writer, Producer, Father of Triplets." It's the best business card I've ever had and really fun to hand out.

Meanwhile, Barbara, Braden, Carter, Jackson, Geno, and Hilda are going to a park in West Hollywood. Afterwards, they're trying out the fun equipment at a place called Tumble Time, which will become a regular destination.

I miss the boys. I won't get home until after they've gone to sleep.

*February 2, 1996*

The boys are barely a year old when we learn that actor Scott Bakula is making a TV movie in which he plays a single guy who suddenly has to take care of a baby. The movie, alternately called *The Bachelor's Baby* and *Here Comes the Son*, is casting for the baby. Somebody tells Barbara, "Oh, you have triplets—you should get them into show business." So Barbara and Geno take all three to an audition in Burbank.

Barb returns home from her first (and last) day as a "stage mother" exhausted and disappointed. The producer explains that, while it's nice we have *fraternal* triplets who definitely look like brothers, the production is looking for *identical* twins or triplets so the babies can be rotated in and out of scenes and always appear to be the same baby. No worries. The boys get paid for their trouble. Fifty dollars each for a minimum of eight hours at $6.25 per hour minus taxes—$45.77 net each. First paycheck. Age one. This is promising.

Barb has arranged cushions and pillows in one corner of the family room next to the sofa to make a "comfy corner" for the boys. When they toddle over and flop down, bury their heads in the pillows, roll over and giggle, Barb writes, "My heart melts. There just isn't anything more adorable and inviting than these happy guys."

Two pieces of equipment are key to managing with triplets. In the early days, it's the Podee bottle. Most parents know that you're never supposed to "prop a bottle" with a baby, meaning never balance a bottle of formula/milk in a baby's mouth and walk away. The baby could gag and choke. But the top of a Podee bottle is attached to a long flexible tube with a nipple on the end. So the baby can easily let it fall out or spit it out. No choking hazard. Thanks to Podee bottles, we're able to safely park our boys in their high chairs, bouncy chairs, cribs, and car seats with hands-free bottles at their sides.

The second piece of equipment is a portable clip-on *seat* with a tray that can be attached to the edge of any table. The suggestion that we buy and carry three of these with us at all times came from another triplet mom. As we begin taking our toddlers out into the world, especially to restaurants, we discover how essential these seats are. If the establishment doesn't have three high chairs, or they don't have three high chairs available when we arrive, we're out of luck. Not anymore. Lifesaver.

Barb notes that after we put the boys down for their morning nap from 9:30 a.m. to 11:00 a.m., we often go back to bed ourselves. And frequently, her notes indicate, this is when we "enjoy the fireplace." Since there's no fireplace in our bedroom, this is obviously a euphemism for ... enjoying the fireplace.

### April 15, 1996

For the first time in our lives, we have three *dependents* we can claim on our tax return. Could it be there's a silver lining in these diaper-filled clouds?

I start looking at how we pay taxes, who pays taxes, and where our tax dollars go. As mentioned earlier, I've always believed taxes are an inevitable necessity, even as conservatives tirelessly "frame" them as a bad thing. Taxes, who pays them, and how we spend what's collected reveals a lot about who we are, what we value, and what we're committed to as a nation.

In the 1996 US budget, for example, we'll spend the most on Social Security (22 percent); Medicare and Medicaid is next (17 percent); defense (16 percent), interest on the debt (16 percent); domestic discretionary spending, such as health, education, housing, energy, food, and agriculture (16 percent); "other" (12 percent), and international affairs (1 percent). (Source: Govinfo.gov/content/pkg/BUDGET-1996)

Mike Lofgren, an author and a Republican, has written incisively about taxes and budgeting, including a number of related realities, myths, and deceptions. Mr. Lofgren was a congressional staff member for twenty-eight years, serving on both the House and Senate Budget committees. When he left government service, he wrote a powerful essay on Truthout.org titled, "Goodbye to All That: Reflections of a GOP Operative Who Left the Cult." In the essay, Lofgren recalls: "When I began work on Capitol Hill in 1983, President Ronald Reagan adopted policies devised by his young budget director, David Stockman, who came up with what he called a 'magic asterisk' in his documents to show that future deficits could be imagined out of existence" by simply placing an asterisk next to potential, future budget cuts. "This deception," he observes, "allowed the Reagan Administration to push through steep tax cuts and vast military increases," presumably while pointing to the "magic asterisks."

"Over President Reagan's two terms," Lofgren explains, "America's gross federal debt nearly tripled. Republicans don't like to talk about this. They like to call Democrats 'tax and spend Democrats.' But Republicans have been budgeting with the 'magic asterisk' and driving up deficits ever since Reagan."

In other words, with their "magic asterisk," the Republicans were saying to themselves, "We're going to explode the deficit by giving rich people a tax cut and spending more on defense but, if anyone insists on cutting costs, they *could* cut the lines in the budget that have an asterisk by them." Welcome to "Magical Budget Thinking."

Lofgren later expanded on his essay in a book, *The Party Is Over: How Republicans Went Crazy, Democrats Became Useless, and the Middle Class Got Shafted,* pointing out that modest tax increases by both President George H. W. Bush and President Clinton effectively "refuted the Republican assertion that even the smallest tax increase would ruin the economy." It blew a hole in their *framing*.

"Republicans have been remarkably successful in delinking taxes from fiscal policy, 'framing' taxes as a distasteful personal burden unconnected to widely-desired public goods like roads, food-safety inspections, or clean water," Lofgren writes. "Instead, they claim that reducing taxes will spur so much investment the cuts will 'pay for themselves.' Three decades of evidence have shown this claim to be false..."

"Working for Republicans," Lofgren concludes, "I learned the hard way that expecting the [Republican] party to restrain the deficit, let alone balance the budget is, in Samuel Johnson's words, 'the triumph of hope over experience.'"

(Unfortunately, in 2001, as our boys are turning six, George W. Bush will follow the example of Mr. Reagan, not his father, Lofgren recalls. "[W's] policies turned a $236 billion budget *surplus* he inherited in 2000 into a $459 billion deficit in 2008, while in those same eight years doubling the national debt." That's a $659 billon swing in the wrong direction, which would have horrified fiscally conservative Republicans in the past. By contrast, when President Obama took office on January 20, 2009, according to the Congressional Budget Office (CBO), the projection for the deficit Obama inherited was $1.2 trillion and 9.8 percent of GDP. Five years later, the CBO projected the federal deficit would be $492 billion, down from $1.2 trillion, and just 2.8 percent of GDP, down from 9.8 percent. This five-year reduction under President Obama ranks as the largest and fastest reduction of the deficit since the end of World War II more than seventy years before. Yep. That's what you get with "tax and spend Democrats.")

The bottom line: "Trickle Down Economics"—the distribution of wealth to big corporations and the very rich in hopes it will trickle down to benefit ordinary workers—has never worked. America will be rebuilt by restoring the middle class, not by continuing to favor the moneyed class.

In the America we're leaving to our children, vital pieces of our infrastructure—roads, bridges, schools, water systems—are failing and urgently need repair. Other essential pieces of infrastructure need to be created or expanded—rural broadband internet connectivity, investment in clean energy production, a nationwide smart electric grid. The money to pay for these things can be found by requiring the super-rich and our largest corporations to pay their fair share of taxes. This may necessitate a thorough revision of the US tax code and spending millions more to enable the Internal Revenue Service (IRS) to enforce the new code, but it must be done.

*April 29, 1996*

Unearthed: A handwritten note from Dr. Friedman recording the boys' measurements: Jackson: Age: 15 months. Weight: 24.7 pounds. Height: 32.5—Head Circumference: 47. Braden: Age: 15 months. Weight 23.10 pounds. Height: 31.5—Head Circumference: 48. Carter: Age: 15 months. Weight: 26.8 pounds. Height: 33—Head Circumference: 49.

In my search for a "real job," I'm being considered for the position of vice president of the Travel Channel in Atlanta. The current VP, Dalton Delan, is moving to the Sundance Channel. With some trepidation, Barbara and I are flying across the country, eager for some peace and quiet as we explore this opportunity. At this point, we've been away from the babies for only one night—in Santa Barbara to attend the ceremony honoring Michael Douglas. Atlanta is our first extended trip away—three nights—leaving Geno and Hilda to hold down the fort. We're looking forward to staying in a hotel and sleeping in. When we're awakened at 6:00 a.m. by the sound of children playing in the room next door, we're upset then realize we miss our boys.

It's a busy visit. There are interviews with Human Resources and executives and meetings with realtors to look at houses. While I'm being evaluated by the Travel Channel folks, we're trying to imagine what family life would be like in Atlanta.

A week or so later, the headhunter calls to say the Travel Channel is hiring someone else. For a moment, I'm disappointed until I learn the Discovery Channel is buying Travel and moving everybody to Baltimore. Travel wasn't offering me a contract, so we could easily have been left stranded in Atlanta. Thank goodness for unanswered prayers.

*May 28, 1996*

I woke up this morning singing a line from a Roger Miller song: "Do the mornings still come early / Are the nights not long enough?"

Staring at me through morning eyes, Barbara answers: "Yes."

But it's better than the first year. And the guys are starting to drink from cups!

*July 9, 1996*

Bottles have served us well, but now the guys are drinking exclusively from cups and relishing the experience. Some of the contents end up on their trays or on the floor, but they're getting good at this newfound skill. They're also talking. Jackson says, "Banana." Braden says, "Bubble." Carter says, "Ball" as he takes it from his brother.

The mother of triplets records a tender, nostalgic observation: "They're not babies anymore; they're toddlers. And there's no going back to those precious early days." She means those precious, overwhelming, sleepless days.

*August 17, 1996*

Remembering my dad on what would have been his eighty-eighth birthday. We're at Beverly Glen Park with the boys, enjoying the swings, the slide, a climbing structure. The triplets are energetic and adventurous and making the most of it all.

An older gentleman approaches me. "Are you the father of the triplets?" he asks with a heavy Eastern European accent. "Yes, I am," I answer. He smiles. "You are a very wealthy man," he says and then walks away. So true.

*August 31, 1996*

We're pushing the boys up Stanley Hills Drive in two strollers—the double and the single—as we and/or the nannies do twice each day. The boys love it. They're getting a glimpse of the world around them. Today, they're chanting, "Bunnies . . . bunnies . . . bunnies," as we pass a point on the walk where there's an empty cage. Many walks ago, there were bunnies in this cage, which the boys loved seeing and obviously remember. At one point when we passed the cage, there were grown bunnies and baby bunnies. That was exciting.

Then, one day when we passed the cage, we noticed it was open, and the bunnies were all gone. We were surprised; the boys were disappointed, and we haven't seen any bunnies for weeks. We're assuming the worst. This is coyote country. And today, we assume the guys' cries for "bunnies" are merely an expression of their naïve and endearing optimism.

But then, on our way back down the hill, at the very spot where the empty cage is, the very spot where there haven't been any bunnies for weeks, suddenly the boys are pointing and shouting, "Bunnies . . . bunnies!"

And there they are. Only now, the family of bunnies is scampering around in the bushes, plain as day, roaming free. The boys are thrilled, and we're appreciating the power of naïve optimism.

*September 21, 1996*

Barb writes: "The boys are fussy, needy, and cranky."

Which also happens to be the name of the worst law firm in Los Angeles.

Toddlers get colds. They have runny noses. They wake up with fevers. All three of the boys have had roseola, which is caused by a herpes virus and comes with a fever and a rash. No wonder they're fussy, needy, and cranky.

Sometimes, of course, even when they're perfectly well, kids need comforting. Whenever they're feeling needy, a few minutes of holding, rocking, back rubbing, and cuddling by one of us usually restores their cheerfulness and sense of well-being. They let us know when they need to be held, and we oblige gladly. The gratification that comes from being the holder, rocker, or cuddler is always delicious.

One rule we follow with the triplets: Never put a baby down to pick up another. Which means don't put down a quiet baby to pick up one that's crying. Because they quickly learn that, by crying, they can attract attention for themselves and take attention away from their sibling. So we comfort the crying boy by checking on him and, if need be, picking him up later.

In moments of exasperation, we remind ourselves of something we learned in our triplet support group: You're always working six months out. Which means that whatever behavior pattern is being created today is what you'll be dealing with in six months. If the boy uses a tantrum to demand what he wants, and gets it, then we'll be seeing more tantrums in the future. On the other hand, if we don't give in to the child's hysterical behavior and let him know he's not going to get what he wants by screaming, we have an opportunity to begin to shift his behavior. We let our boys know that they need to ask politely for what they want. We're trying to teach them appropriate behavior for this moment and six months from now.

## DIVING IN

*March 1997 – Year Three*

Our toddlers are twenty-seven months old. See those guys over there, drinking from cups? Those are two-year-olds!

With two nannies on the payroll during the day and our boys sleeping through the night, we're both working, and the house is humming. The only hitch is we have to move. The house we've been renting in Laurel Canyon has been sold out from under us; I'm in the middle of producing the 3rd *Blockbuster Entertainment Awards*, and we're moving to a house in the Encino Hills. The Encino house has a big gated backyard with guard towers at the corners. Kidding about the guard towers. It does have a long covered patio. We need to check out the local school; the boys will be going to kindergarten in less than three years. Hell-o!

*Spring 1998*

The triplets are three years old and eating a lot of food, which is to say pretty much everything we put in front of them. To keep track of who's eating what and answer the ever-present question, "Whose plate is this?" we've added color-coding to their dishes. Braden has a blue plate and blue cup, Carter gets green, and Jackson gets red.

"Hey, Carter didn't eat his rice!" How do we know? There's still a pile of rice on the green plate.

"Jackson, do you want more juice?" Why do we ask? The red cup is empty. It works. They've got their own dishes. They like it.

Now that the guys are three, we think, *great, the terrible twos are over*. So we stop at a family restaurant for a bite to eat. "Casady party of five" is now a reality. The boys are now big enough to sit at a table with booster seats, so we occupy a booth by a window without needing high chairs or clip-on seats. We must collect the silverware, however, because the fellas like to use the utensils as drumsticks. If we don't collect the utensils, it's going to sound like a scene from *The Lion King* in here. Barb passes out the crayons she carries with her in her purse so the guys can draw on the paper placemats. She also dumps the little sugar and artificial sweetener packets onto the table and asks the boys to sort them by color. We order some drinks. We're good.

We're good until the boys decide they need something more exciting to do. Before we can stop them, they're literally climbing up the blinds on the window next to our table. We pull them down, but they climb back up. We're in a public place, and it looks like we have three monkeys with us.

We command them to stop, but they're having too much fun. This wouldn't happen with one three-year-old. Add a second three-year-old to encourage the first one, and you might have a situation. Add a third one—this dynamic is becoming familiar—and you have mayhem. And they won't stop. They *are* monkeys. Commands are not effective. We call the waitress over and tell her we're leaving before we get thrown out. We gather up the boys and make our escape.

On our way out, I tell Barbara: "Honey, I love our kids, but if you ever leave me, I'm right behind you!"

We're never taking the kids to a restaurant again. At home, we're up to our eyeballs in diapers as well as childproof locks and pressure gates to keep the boys from getting into everything. It's a little easier than the first two years, but it's virtually impossible to find meaningful adult time. There's so much work to be done—cleaning, washing, cooking, playdates, games, doctor appointments, birthday parties, shopping—that even when you do it as a couple, you feel like a single parent.

*Summer 1998*

Barbara's busy designing a condo near the racetrack in Del Mar for a client who just sold his company for millions. He wants it "turnkey," which means Barb is selecting, buying, and installing everything, including all the furnishings, TVs, dishes, silverware, cookware, towels, linens, soap, toilet paper, bathrobe, bedroom slippers, even a toothbrush and toothpaste. Del Mar is over an hour south; the job is taking a lot of time, and Barb is gone a lot.

To fill their days, I'm taking the boys to a summer camp in the Valley. The camp requires that they be "out" of diapers which, thankfully, they are. Talk about a raise; we feel like we've gotten a *promotion*. As we pay our final bill, the Dydee Diaper Service informs us that our count for three-plus years is over thirty-seven thousand diapers.

Today, when I pick up the boys at summer camp, I'm shocked to see the name "Cassidy Carter" on the checkout sheet. Our last name is sometimes misspelled, but at summer camp? Upon closer examination, I see there's also a "Jackson Carter" on the list. What the hell? Figuring that something's wrong, I inquire at the office and am told that "Cassidy Carter" and "Jackson Carter" are twins. My head is about to explode. And, ready for this—they were born on January 8, 1995, one day after our boys. (Years later, the confusion will arise again at the pediatric dentist office where our kids' charts become confused with the Carter twins, and again during baseball tryouts at Encino Little League. At one point, while watching Jackson Carter try out, Barbara turns to the gentleman next to her and says, "We have a son named Jackson and a son named Carter; I'd like to meet this boy's parents." To which the man replies, "That would be me." It turns out that Tony Carter is not only the father of the twins but also the owner of Carter Hardware where Barb frequently shops.

One night at the end of the summer, as Barbara and I are putting the boys to bed, Jackson says, "I don't like summer." When Barb asks him why, Jackson says, "I don't like summer because you're not here." Barbara's heart breaks. Fortunately, it won't be long before her job is finished.

## Sundays with Russert

As a DINK couple, we used to sleep late on Sunday mornings. No more. Now, we get up at the crack of dawn on Sunday and, while the boys are sitting in their high chairs learning to eat and throw solid food, we watch Tim Russert, the longest-serving host of the longest-running show on television, NBC's *Meet the Press*. We could watch cartoons and other morning shows for kids, but we don't. We're starved for any morsel of an adult experience we can find. The boys don't seem to mind Tim Russert, and we get to spend a little "adult time" thinking about the outside world.

One Sunday, after *Meet the Press*, we're at a toddler birthday party with our friends, the Haydens. They've hired a guy in a big, purple dinosaur suit—a Barney—to entertain the kids. All the other kids are going crazy. Our guys don't even notice the purple guy. Finally, Jim comes over and says, "Gee, we went to all the trouble to hire Barney for the party, but your kids don't seem to know who he is. Don't they watch *Barney* on Sunday mornings?" Barb looks at Jim through tired eyes and says, "No, but they'd get really excited if they saw someone in a Tim Russert suit!" (Many years later in Des Moines, Iowa, Barb had a chance to share this story with Tim Russert. He laughed out loud.)

## The Market Disaster

We're at Whole Foods in Encino. I'm pushing one cart with the three guys in it while Barb collects food in another. If we don't contain the boys, they're like wallpaper—everywhere. I notice a big display of coffee. We like coffee. We need coffee. Intravenously. I push my basket toward the coffee. The boys are standing up messing with each other. As I reach out for a bag of coffee beans, I let go of the handle for a split second.

The boys shift to one side to see what I'm doing, and the cart tips over, spilling them onto the concrete floor with the worst sound I've ever heard as a parent. *Crack!*

Braden face-plants and comes up bellowing with a bloody nose. Carter and Jackson are crying. At first, it's impossible to tell who is hurt or how badly.

I'm horrified and embarrassed.

Suddenly, a store manager and a couple of other employees appear to help us assess the situation and usher us upstairs to an office. They call 911 and some paramedics show up. Braden appears to have the most serious injury, to his nose. The paramedics want to put him in a neck brace, strap him down on a board, and transport him to the ER in Tarzana. We tell them we'll take the boys to urgent care in Encino.

Barbara is amazingly calm. At urgent care, an ER doctor is concerned that Braden may have a broken nose. While I wait with Carter and Jackson, Barbara takes Braden back to get an X-ray. The tech needs Barbara to hold Braden absolutely still, face down on the table. Braden's three. Three-year-old boys don't know from "absolutely still." They know "constantly moving" (like sharks) or "asleep." Frustrated that Braden keeps moving, the tech says they need to put Braden in a straitjacket for the X-ray. "No," Barbara says. "That's not going to happen." Putting an injured child in a straitjacket for a medical procedure is guaranteed to psychologically mar the child for life, isn't it?

From the ER, Barb calls our pediatrician for advice. Dr. Fred is clear. In all his years, he's never seen a child under the age of six with a broken bone. Then he gets to the point: "Ask the doctor what he's going to do if the X-ray shows that Braden has a broken nose."

"There's nothing we can do," the doctor says.

"Fine," Barb says. "We're going home."

Braden's nose isn't broken. The scratches are healing. But the boys are traumatized, to be sure, and so are we. The worst feeling in the world is knowing you did something, or didn't do something, that resulted in your kids being harmed.

### 156 Weeks In

Birthdays in our house are not only a rite of passage but also a celebration of survival. Practically from the moment they all came home—or at least after we survived "Where's Marta?"—they have basked in the warm, loving glow of Genoveva Martinez Suarez, our lead nanny. She's been caring for the triplets since they were about eight weeks old.

The boys are now more than 156 weeks old, and as the weeks have turned into months and years, we've come to see how truly great Geno is. At various hours, sometimes after coming home from a rare evening out, we'll go into the nursery to check on the guys. And there they are, wrapped snuggly in their little cotton blankets, resting blissfully on their sides, heads perfectly propped up, as if they've been gently placed there by angels.

The angel is Geno.

Now, one month and thirteen days after their third birthday, Geno is leaving us. She and her two sons, Gabriel and Armando, are moving to Tennessee to live with family. Gabriel is married and has two baby daughters of his own. Armando, sixteen, who arrived recently from Santa Cruz, Mexico, is struggling with adolescence. Geno and her family have grown weary of living in downtown Los Angeles. Rents are high, and they're tired of putting up with the ever-present threat of gangs.

Geno went from being our nighttime nanny to our lead daytime nanny, cheerfully, lovingly, and tirelessly caring for our three boys, usually six days a week, for three years. She saw them start to eat solid food, walk, talk, and emerge as three distinct personalities. She cared for them and traveled with us when we had to travel, always providing the tender, reassuring, loving care day and night that she provided in the wee hours when we first needed her so desperately. This year, she saw them start nursery school.

Genoveva has given us and our children the enormous gift of loving and caring for them as she loved and cared for her own children.

We love Geno, and we will miss her. We're telling her: Don't be surprised if the three boys you have helped nurture from infancy through their toddler and preschool years come knocking on your door someday. One thing is certain: they will always remember you.

We give her a framed quotation that we've had translated into Spanish. It reads: "100 years from now, it will not matter what your bank account was, or the sort of house you lived in, or the kind of car your drove, but the world may be different because you were important in the life of a child. Thank you, Genoveva, for being important in the lives of our three children."

## The Ten-Year Deduction

We're having dinner with our longtime friend Marlo Bendau, a brilliant documentary filmmaker who was one of the wildly generous hosts of our baby shower. Apropos of nothing, Marlo asks, "Have you guys taken the ten-year deduction?" To which we reply, "What's the ten-year deduction? Is that a tax thing?" "No," she says, "it's an *age* thing. You take ten years off your age by simply saying you were born ten years later than you were." If you were born in 1947, you say you were born in 1957. Easy to remember. No paperwork. You just take the ten-year deduction in your mind, and you're done. As far as everyone is concerned, except your doctor, your spouse, and the DMV, you're automatically ten years younger.

Okay. But why would we do that?

Oh, wait! We have little kids.

When our kids start school at age five, I'll be fifty-two and Barb will be forty-nine, easily ten or fifteen years older than most of the other parents in the school. Do we want people to think we're our kids' parents or their grandparents?

We're taking the ten-year deduction.

From now on, whenever the kids ask us when we were born or how old we are, we lie. Because when kids are little-little, we know if we tell them our real ages, they'll blurt it out to their friends and teachers and who knows who; they won't appreciate our reasons for wanting to be ten years younger.

Oh, and by the way, show business is an ageist business. How old you are matters. Asking people how old they are in a job interview is illegal, of course, but it happens. A few weeks after taking the ten-year deduction, I'm being interviewed by a producer who wants me to write a book for him. He asks me how old I am. Totally illegal question. I'm forty-nine, but I'm taking the deduction. So I say, "I'm not really a thirty-nine-year-old writer-producer, but I play one in Hollywood." He looks at me and says, "Oh." He thinks I've just told him I'm thirty-nine. It's working.

*Saving a School*

Uh-oh. The boys are soon-to-be-preschoolers, and we still haven't checked out the local elementary school. All we know is that Lanai Road Elementary sits in a lovely, parklike setting at the edge of the neighborhood below us and it used to be one of the top schools in the Los Angeles Unified School District (LAUSD).

We're invited to a meeting to talk about the school and arrive at a neighbor's house to find about a hundred other parents in attendance. We learn the school has seriously deteriorated in recent years. The principal is on a retirement track and apparently no longer interested in the work of delivering a quality public education. Teachers are being ignored. There aren't enough books for the students. A fairly large percentage of the student body is being bused in from other parts of Los Angeles because the neighborhood has changed. Many of the surrounding houses are occupied by "empty nesters" whose children have long since flown the coop. Parents of school-age kids who do live in the area are opting to send their children to pricey private schools at the top of the hill along Mulholland Drive.

We believe in public schools. We're not about to do private school times three.

And the verdict is that our "used to be a top-notch public elementary school" is on its knees. The mom who organized the meeting has two kids who are younger than ours. She has been out pushing her kids around the neighborhood in a stroller, casually conducting a survey. She admits that the "empty nester" neighbors across the street from us spilled the beans on our family. "Oh, yeah, the Casadys have three toddlers."

After months of sleuthing, this farsighted neighbor, Jeannie Kamm, has figured out that there are enough kids in the neighborhood to fill a kindergarten class with five-year-olds in 2000, when our kids will be five, and another class in 2001. Secretly, I think it will probably take a generation to turn around a neighborhood school, but we instantly write a check for a hundred dollars to join the parent group determined to turn around Lanai Road Elementary.

And I was wrong about how long it would take. Over the next three years, this energetic collective of parents will completely transform the school. By the time our boys are five years old and ready to go to kindergarten, Lanai Road Elementary is on its way to becoming a California Distinguished, Federal Blue Ribbon elementary school.

## The Cat That Went to School

While we work on Lanai Road Elementary, the boys are going to preschool at the Stephen Wise School up the hill, off Mulholland Drive. And Lucy, our white cat with the piercing blue eyes, is missing. We haven't seen her since the beginning of spring break, and the boys want us to put up posters with Lucy's picture on them all over the neighborhood. We live in the hills in a neighborhood where we hear coyotes at night and see them during the day in our backyard. And we have a white cat. We think "missing" is a nice way of saying "Lucy is toast."

But the guys insist, so we're making posters, and not just little 8.5" x 11" ones that we can print out of our computer. No, these are 18" x 24" jobs with a big picture of Lucy pasted on them. They're movie posters. Works of art. And we drive around in the van stapling them up on phone poles and wherever else we can.

The boys are convinced the posters are going to work, but we have no idea where Lucy is and, honestly, think this is an exercise in futility. Can you spell "coyote lunch?" But as a parent, you can't *say* that. You have to be optimistic or pretend that you are.

Mind you, Lucy has a habit of getting in vehicles. One day, when Barbara was driving out to Burbank, Lucy suddenly appeared in the car—a stowaway. Barb almost drove back to the house, but that would have made her late, so she left Lucy in the car with the window cracked open. Another time, I was driving to work and Lucy suddenly appeared behind my seat. I drove her back home. On another occasion, Lucy climbed into the back of a truck that delivered some mattresses to the house. Several hours later, the driver calls to ask if the white cat in the back of his truck might be ours. She slept in the truck overnight, took a trip to Dana Point, and was returned by the nice driver the next day.

The week goes by with no sign of Lucy. Then, on Sunday, the phone rings.

"Did you lose a white cat with piercing blue eyes?" a woman asks.

"Yes, we did."

"My daughter saw your poster, and she thinks she has seen your cat."

"Really? Where?"

"Up at the school."

"Oh my God," I say. "Thank you so much! And please thank your daughter for us. What can we do to thank you?"

*Click.*

On Monday morning. I drive the boys to school. The boys pile out with their little backpacks on and head for their classroom.

I get out and look around. I see a maintenance man.

"Excuse me, have you seen a white cat with piercing blue eyes around here?"

"You mean that one?" he says, pointing off into the distance.

And there she is. It's Lucy.

She starts running toward me.

In slow motion. Which I think is odd.

And the music from *Chariots of Fire* is playing.

It's like a scene from *Lassie* with the wrong music. And the wrong animal.

Lucy jumps into the van!

I'm stunned. Posters work. Cat found.

We conclude that Lucy must have hopped into the van on the Friday morning before spring break, and when the boys got out, she hopped out of the van. We assume she roamed the campus, frightened small rodents, found something to eat, and hid well at night until we returned to find her.

Lessons learned: Listen to your kids. Do what's right. Make posters. Never give up hope.

*Chapter 5*

# CHOICE MAN

> *I came to parenting the way most of us do—knowing nothing*
> *and trying to learn everything.*
> —MAYIM BIALIK, ACTRESS AND NEUROSCIENTIST

The minute you have a child, you become familiar with dread, with a fear that something terrible might happen to your child. It starts the instant a child is born and lasts forever. It's inescapable. You do a lot of things to prevent bad things from happening to your children, but things still happen.

### *April 1999—Missing*

At four, the boys are old enough to understand commands like "Stop!" before they step off the curb into traffic. "Come here!" works. But three energetic four-year-old preschoolers require watching.

About three weeks ago, Legoland opened in Carlsbad, a couple of hours south of us. Legos are very popular in our house, so we're going! And we're going to be extra cautious. I call my eldest brother, Derek, who lives in La Jolla, not far from Carlsbad, to ask whether he can join us. We want one adult per child. He agrees.

The six of us cruise around Legoland, one adult per triplet. It's like watching the water if you're a lifeguard, only here you watch the kid.

Legoland is filled with lots of assorted attractions and colorful structures made of Legos, including a giant dinosaur. We have lunch at a place that has an astonishing Lego city the kids can experience up close.

After lunch, we discover a huge climbing structure where the guys can crawl around inside a massive labyrinth. Derek, Barbara, and I sit out front, keeping an eye on the boys as they disappear inside the maze with other kids.

The fun way out of the maze is a slide that comes out the front of the structure. Woo-hoo! Here comes Braden. Then Jackson. A long beat, but no Carter.

"Where's Carter?"

Braden and Jackson don't know. Derek moves closer to look inside, and I try to climb in, but the passages are too small for an adult. I check, and there's no exit in the back. Kids can only go in and come out the front. Barbara and I hold hands with Braden and Jackson, while Derek keeps looking for Carter.

We're worried. We've heard horror stories about young children being kidnapped from theme parks.

We spot a security guard and tell him one of our kids is missing. We describe Carter, his age, height, what he's wearing. The security guard calls it in on his radio.

I pick up Jackson and hold him tight as we continue to pace around the structure. Barbara is holding Braden, calling Carter's name. Derek checks the structure again and the surrounding area.

I am so scared I don't know what to do. I'm afraid my fear is palpable, that Jackson may be feeling it as I hold him close.

Twenty, maybe thirty minutes go by. The scariest twenty to thirty minutes of our lives as parents. We have one-on-one coverage for our kids, and we've lost one. How could this happen?

After what seems like an eternity, the security guard appears.

"We found him."

We hear voices crackling back and forth on the guard's radio. "Blond." "Green shirt." "Says his name is Carter."

We breathe a sigh of relief like no other.

"Where is he?"

They've found Carter halfway across the park looking at the model Lego city we saw at lunch.

We realize the climbing attraction is open to the rest of the park on the front side and isn't fenced or separated in any way. Carter tells us he came down the slide and just kept on running. He wanted to go see that Lego city again. It's at Legoland that we learn Carter is what they call "fleet of foot." Whenever we go to a local park, if we let Carter out of his car seat first, before we can unload his brothers, he's off and running by himself, chasing a balloon or something. Note to self: Gotta watch him.

Our accident at Whole Foods taught us that shopping with little kids can be crazy-making and dangerous.

One day, when I'm shopping alone, the checker asks me why I'm buying so much food. I tell her we have triplets. She says, "Oh my, triplets! Is your wife a young mother?" I say, "She is now."

Barbara's also a fearless shopper. Barbara takes all three guys shopping for shoes because the shoe store gives customers a meaningful discount *if* you bring in *all the siblings* together. What they haven't considered is triplet boys and what we call the "puppies in a pile" or "monkeys on the blinds" factor. Barb describes it this way: While she and the clerk are fitting one boy, the other two are spinning the sock rack to see how fast they can make it go or climbing the shelves and pulling down shoeboxes or pushing the salesman's stool across the carpet like a race car at the Indy 500. Or they're wrestling in the middle of the store. It's harrowing for Barb and the clerk, but hey—she gets that discount.

We're in Toys "R" Us shopping for toys. And we're noticing things you're not necessarily aware of until you have kids. For example, most of the toys have age-appropriate markings. "For Ages 3-4" or "Ages 11-14." Thanks to the US Consumer Product Safety Commission, we see myriad other warnings: "Choking Hazard: Small parts not for children under 3 years." "Parent Supervision Required." "Caution: Contains Boron. May be harmful if eaten." "May generate dust containing lead." Dozens and dozens of regulations ensure the purity of the formula and food we buy, the safety of the bottles and car seats children use, the toys they play with, the clothes and pajamas they wear.

In my father's America, fewer products and foods were regulated. More regulations came along when my brothers and I were growing up. Seat belts are a good example. When we were kids, cars didn't have seat belts, and there was no such thing as a *car seat* for babies and toddlers.

Historically, regulations have been put in place to save lives, prevent illness, and assure product quality and safety. But during the past four decades, Republican administrations have pushed for the deregulation of virtually every sector of American life. President Ronald Reagan championed getting rid of regulations; both Presidents Bush pleased their bases by eliminating what they called "meddlesome regulations" that "hurt the job creators" and "harm the economy." Yet, despite the anti-regulation fervor, research shows that, in fact, regulations save lives, prevent people from becoming sick, reduce the number of days people miss work and, in doing so, *save* billions of dollars.

For example, the Office of Management and Budget (OMB) found that over the last decade, the benefits of Environmental Protection Agency (EPA) regulations vastly outweighed their costs—up to $706 billion in benefits compared to up to $65 billion in costs.* That's a sizeable return for doing what's right. Still, "regulations are bad" remains a favorite chant of conservatives, even though they and their loved ones' lives have been saved by seat belts, three-point car seats, clean water standards, warnings on drug labels, food inspections, the abolition of dangerous pesticides, and more. Regulations are "greed control." Intelligent regulations put people over profits. *(Source: *2017 Draft Report to Congress on the Benefits and Costs of Federal Regulations and Agency Compliance with the Unfunded Mandates Reform Act.*)

*Choice Man*

In the tumult of raising young children, having some "regulations" isn't a terrible idea. While raising her five boys, my mother used to tell us she was just "trying to bring order out of chaos." If you have young kids or grandkids, the following advice is worth the price of this book. It's one of the main reasons we were able to survive raising triplets, and it can work in any family with two or more kids. It's a simple practice called "Choice Person," or in our house, "Choice Man."

We heard about Choice Man from one of the moms in our triplet support group. Yes, there is such a thing as a triplet support group. The group is a safe place where bleary-eyed parents can meet, share their woes, commiserate, complain, and cry, away from their children, in hopes of finding the strength to go back home and parent for a few more days.

Choice Person is brilliant. In simple rotation, one child gets to be the Choice Person each day. On his/her day, Choice Person gets to sit where he/she wants to sit in the car, go on a special outing with Mom and Dad, pick which video or TV show to watch, decide what's for dessert, choose which book to read at bedtime, and so on. The next day, another child is Choice Person with all the same rights.

In our house, we call it "Choice Man." We use it every day. The boys like it because they know it doesn't matter who is Choice Man today; their day will come. If Carter is Choice Man today, Braden knows he'll be Choice Man tomorrow, and Jackson knows he'll be Choice Man in two days. The kids give it up to whoever is the day's Choice Man. It works beautifully. We write the rotation on a calendar so that we can check to see whose day it is. Important Rule: You can't trade Choice Man days. No trading, buying, or selling. Simple rotation. Becoming Choice Man (Person) is guaranteed. Your day will come.

The Choice Man system gives the boys a chance to express their unique desires as well as experience being favored for a day. At the same time, it allows them to share what they're interested in with their brothers. And it virtually eliminates arguments between the kids because arguments are about control. Choice Man gives the child control over most of the things he cares about on his day. The kids get it, and it's part of our family's rhythm.

Our dear friends and comrades in Tripletdom, Betsy and Richard Breen, have two girls and a boy. So, of course, in their house, this ingenious system is "Choice Person," and it works wonders for them too. One day, Betsy and one of her daughters, who was three or four at the time, were talking about the obvious difference between boys and girls. "Boys have penises, and girls have vaginas," Betsy says. "And what do you have?" she asks her daughter. "I have a vagina, Mommy," her daughter answers. "That's right," Betsy says, "And what does that make you?" Without hesitating, her daughter answers, "That makes me Choice Person!"

### Unique Equals

I'm learning that dads are prone to interpreting events in ways that can be dangerous or inaccurate or both. I call it "Dad Think." Braden, Carter, and Jackson are out on our back patio in Encino with a small basketball and a freestanding, toddler-size basketball hoop. The guys are dancing around, shooting the ball, missing, having fun. Carter gets the ball, steps back, sizes up the hoop, shoots. He's the first to make a basket.

Here's an example of Dad Think. Inner voice, unspoken: *Well, it looks like Carter's going to be the basketball player.* The boys keep playing. Maybe two minutes later. Braden steps back, shoots, makes it. Jackson grabs the ball circles back, shoots and makes a basket.

Oh, wait. I realize something. Their reality is, "If he can do it, so can I." And if Dad keeps his mouth shut, why wouldn't that be true?

Another aha moment. We're in the backyard playing baseball. I'm pitching underhanded. We're working on hand-eye coordination in real time and space. They're taking turns getting a piece of it with a yellow plastic bat, whacking balls toward the neighbor's house. Jackson is at bat. He swings and misses. He throws the bat down and runs into the house.

Dad Think. Inner voice, unspoken: *Damn, I guess Jackson doesn't like baseball.* I pitch to Carter; he smacks it. I pitch to Braden; he smacks it. Carter's ready to bat again when Jackson comes running out of the house. "Hey," he yells, "it's my turn!" As he takes the bat from Carter, I say stupidly, "I thought you didn't want to play." He squares up his stance and says, "I had to pee." And smacks the ball over the fence.

In my mind, I was already looking for another sport for Jackson. He wasn't. He loves baseball as much as his brothers. After reflexively succumbing to Dad Think, I get it. This is important and helpful. I realize that, for the triplets, their assumption about everything they do is, "If he can do it, so can I," because they're the same age, born at the same time, living in the same house, standing on the same ground.

Over time, we'll observe countless examples of this and come to call it our "Theory of Unique Equals." Remember our song, "We are three individuals, one, two, three?" It's true: they are *unique* individuals and, as far as they're concerned, they're also *equal* in ways that wouldn't occur to siblings who are born years apart. As the youngest of five boys, I can attest to this fact. I always felt unique but never "equal."

An important operating principle of our theory is that, if we (and others) don't intervene and create artificial differences between them—who's the oldest, who's the smartest, who's the best at basketball—they will not. On their own, they won't manufacture those differences, because they see themselves as equals. Unique and equal.

From time to time, strangers (mostly) will ask, "Which one is the smartest?" We think to ourselves: *Obviously, not you.* The truth is, and we tell people this, "We don't go there." At this point, the boys don't even know their birth order (they won't find out until they get their driver licenses at sixteen). We don't let them compare their report cards or test scores, though they are very similar. What would be the point of doing that except to create differences between them?

## The Balloon at the Market

When you become a father, you're suddenly not just tuned in to your kids—you're tuned into *all* kids. Kids suddenly show up in a way they didn't when you didn't have any.

One day, I'm at the grocery store near our house that has a small branch of my bank inside. People love having this little teller window at the market. I'm in a line of people waiting to get to the teller window. There are a few people in line behind me. We're all waiting patiently, moving up slowly.

A woman in front of me is with a little boy who's maybe four years old. He has a balloon on a string. I can relate to a four-year-old; we've got three of them. I can also relate to balloons.

The little boy suddenly starts crying. He's inconsolable. The mom is trying to calm him down and waving at the ceiling. I look up and see the boy has lost his balloon. It's up on the ceiling, far above our heads with just the string hanging down. For some reason, maybe because I'm the only person in line reacting to the mother and the boy's distress, she gives me a *What do I do?* look.

I decide to help. This is a job for a dad. I will jump up and grab the string and bring the balloon back down to earth! I'm six foot four with long arms. I can do this. I position myself under the balloon. Now, everybody in line is looking at me. The mom is looking at me. The boy is crying, looking at me. I crouch down and jump as high as I can with outstretched arms reaching for the string. I miss it. The people in line react: "Ohhhh." The boy cries louder. The mom looks even more distressed. I position myself under the balloon again. The expressions on the faces of the people in line are not encouraging. I crouch down and take a deep breath. I spring into the air and touch the string but fall back before I can grab it. The crowd sighs. "Awww!" The kid is still crying. Now, I'm more determined than ever to get his balloon. Why? Because now it's no longer about the kid or the balloon. It's about me looking bad.

I crouch down and spring like I've never sprung before, summoning every fiber of explosive muscle in my legs. This time, I grab the string and bring the balloon down with me! The folks in line cheer and applaud. The boy falls silent as I hand him his balloon and his mom ties the string around his wrist. She thanks me profusely. I turn to leave, figuring I'll come back another time. As I'm walking out, a guy in line yells after me, "Who says white men can't jump?"

## The Country around Us

One evening in 1999, after the boys have gone to bed, I'm reading in the *LA Times* that the American economy is undergoing a major change. Specifically, the rules that governed banking and investment companies in my father's America, most of which survived in the America I grew up in, are being rewritten.

Like so many parents, we're both working to make enough money to raise our family and maybe save a little. We each have simplified employee pension individual retirement accounts (SEP IRAs). These aren't big accounts with big holdings, and we're not exactly sophisticated investors, but we're using some of the money we put away to buy stocks through a brokerage. We know just enough about the economy, big banks, and big investors to know that our investments are insignificant and our access to real wealth at this point is severely limited. If anything, we feel like small parasites on the backs of some larger predators that we hope will kill something that we can eat without being eaten.

We know who the big players are by reading about them in the business section of the paper. I, for one, am intrigued by forces beyond our control that, nonetheless, have an impact on our family, on every family, probably because it seems like so much is beyond my control. Whatever the reason, I'm reading that Goldman Sachs (GS), the giant multinational investment bank that has been in private hands for generations, is going public despite the vehement objections of members of the founding Samuel Sachs family and numerous partners and associates. The company's new co-CEOs, Hank Paulson and Jon Corzine, are taking the company public anyway and, by doing so, will effectively shift the risk from themselves as owners to their shareholders.

Paulson and Corzine are allowed to take Goldman Sachs public because, as our boys approach their fifth birthday and President Clinton approaches the end of his second term, Clinton and the Republicans are passing something called the Financial Services Modernization Act of 1999. This law will thoroughly and effectively do away with restrictions on the integration of banking, insurance, and stock trading that were imposed by the Glass-Steagall Act of 1933. Under Glass-Steagall, one of the central pillars of President Franklin Roosevelt's New Deal, banks, brokerages, and insurance companies were prohibited from entering each other's businesses, and investment banking and commercial banking were kept separate. In other words, the financial industry was *regulated*.

By overturning Glass-Steagall, Clinton and the Republicans are throwing open the door to a long, dark, greed-filled hallway, ushering in a tectonic shift in the way Wall Street conducts business that will occur before our kids enter first grade. (And when the bill is signed, who gets the first pen? Sandy Weill, the chairman and chief executive of mega bank Citigroup.)

Years later, in a much-heralded op-ed piece in the *New York Times*, former GS trader Greg Smith will shine a bright light on how "The Street" changed. Smith, a London-based executive director for Goldman Sachs who oversaw equity derivatives, exposed the change in culture at Goldman after he joined the firm in 2000, shortly after Goldman went public. The big change: Smith says profits were now coming before the interest of clients who were often derided as "Muppets" by people at Goldman. He witnesses and attests to the end of anything resembling "greed control" on Wall Street.

According to Charles M. Elson, a professor of corporate governance at the University of Delaware, "When these firms changed from private partnerships to public companies, the ethos changed dramatically. The notion of client loyalty went out with the old structure." As more and more firms used their own capital in proprietary trading—trading for themselves—Elson says they adopted a "short-term mentality" to make as much money as possible. And of course, massive increases in compensation for traders and stockholders followed.

The market's obsession with short-term greed is nothing new, of course; it certainly played a role in the Great Depression that left lasting scars on my father's America and persistent fears there was going to be another depression. In the America I came up in, the conventional wisdom was there would never be another Great Depression, although no one could ever tell me why.

What does any of this have to do with our children?

It's formational. Our children will have to navigate a drastically different financial landscape than the one we learned to navigate. The new rules, or lack of them, will complicate and disrupt their lives in ways we and, more importantly, they can't even predict. Like good parents, we're dreading what we, and they, may have to face. Even in 1999, I can see we are living with a form of capitalism that has been hijacked by our largest corporations for the benefit of shareholders and billionaires. Is this the America we want for Braden, Carter, and Jackson? Not really.

## *Cowboy Lovemaking*

Meanwhile, we're trying our best to deal with the fact that privacy is hard to come by in a house with three four-year-old boys. Because we continue to have yearnings of the flesh—we're old, but we're not dead—we've come up with something we call Cowboy Lovemaking. Wait. Come back. It's not what you think. Take off the chaps. Step away from the pony.

Cowboy Lovemaking is simple. We go into our room and close the door. We'd lock it, but it's broken, so we prop a chair under the doorknob to brace the door closed. If we're worried the chair won't hold, we slide the dresser against the door like they do in the cowboy movies when the bad guys are trying to bust into the room.

It's Saturday morning. We're having some private time. Trying to "enjoy the fireplace." The chair is propped under the doorknob. The dresser is against the door. The boys are downstairs. They've been told to leave us alone. We hear someone try to open the door. Then, there's a knock.

"Mommy . . . Daddy?"

"Who's there?" we ask.

"Braden."

"What do you want, Braden?"

"Can I come in?"

"No. We'll be down in little while. Go back downstairs with your brothers."

"Can I ask you a question?"

"Okay."

"Do you know how many Pokémon there are?"

"No, Braden, we don't."

"There are 136 Pokémon. Bye!"

We hear the pitter-patter of feet. He's gone. We're laughing.

Oh, the reason the door to our bedroom is broken has to do with a disciplinary incident. The guys were three; they went into our bedroom alone to play, which they're not supposed to do, and locked the door. Our bedroom is not childproofed; it's on the second floor with a window that's open; there are cabinets under the bathroom sinks with who knows what in them; there's a bathtub next to a window that opens onto the roof above the patio. Not a place for three unattended three-year-olds. I pound on the door. "Boys, open the door!" I can hear them giggling and horsing around. "Boys," I bellow, "open the door, now." More giggling.

In the past, we've used the time-honored disciplinary device of counting to three, and it has worked; we've never gotten to three before. The boys always modify their behavior at two. So I say, "Boys, I'm going to count to three, and before I get to three, you need to open the door."

Silence for a moment. Like they're digesting the message. I check the door. Still locked. I repeat: "Boys, open the door!" More sounds of giggling and horsing around inside. I yell "One!" and pause. They're still messing around. I bellow, "Two!" No response. "Open the door," I shout. More giggling. I haven't thought through what to do if they don't open the door, but they're not opening it. I yell, "Three!" Still no response. I take a few steps back in the hall, charge forward, and throw myself at the door as hard as I can. The door explodes open, breaking the lock, and I'm in the room, standing over the boys.

I'll never forget the expressions on their faces. Surprise doesn't quite get it. Shock is closer. Stunned disbelief is more like it. "Let's go," I command, and I march them downstairs. I never had to count to three with my boys after that. And we never repaired the door.

"Trash truck! Trash truck! Trash truck!" The boys stampede toward the front door. Whatever they were doing has been stopped cold by the sound of an approaching trash truck. In the America I grew up in, there were usually three men on a trash truck—a driver and two guys hanging off the back to hoist the large trash cans and empty them into the back of the truck. No more. These trucks have a powerful mechanical arm on the side that grabs the cans, hoists them up, tips them over, and shakes them out. One man—the driver—does it all. It's pretty exciting. One truck comes for the black cans filled with trash and headed for a landfill. Another truck collects the blue cans filled with recyclable cans, bottles, cardboard, and plastic. Yet another giant truck comes for the green cans filled with yard waste.

The trash truck frenzy has been happening every week on trash day since the boys were three. The triplets fire out the front door and sit side by side at the top of the steps with a perfect view of the street, the cans, and the trucks. They're close enough to feel the power of the trucks and see the cans going up and into the truck but far enough away to be safe. In terms of trash truck viewing, these are 50-yard-line seats.

All three are fascinated with the trucks and the trash-collecting business. The drivers seem pleased to have the adoring audience. Carter has taken an extraordinary interest in our trash. He's been studying the cans for weeks on the way to and from school. This morning, he's intent on borrowing the neighbor's green can because its wheels have "treads" and the wheels on our green can don't. He clearly feels the wheels with treads are superior to the smooth ones. So, on the way to school, at ten minutes before 9:00 a.m., Carter asks Barbara to call the neighbor and ask whether we can borrow their green can. "For two trash days," he insists. The neighbor agrees. We are ever grateful for the kindness of neighbors.

It's bedtime. The boys want to play a game they call "Turning Things Around." Tonight, Braden begins with, "Girls have peenies, and boys don't." Mommy says, "Does that mean you're a girl?" The three answer emphatically in unison, "No!" Mommy offers, "What if boys had peenies and girls had peenies?" Jackson answers, "It would be a peenie world."

One day in the playroom. Braden is pretending to be the giant killer squid from *Godzilla*, hiding behind a stack of pillows. Jackson approaches, Braden rears up and screeches a fearsome roar. Jackson falls back, pulls off his pajama bottoms, and runs away. Barbara asks, "Why did you take your pants off?" Jackson answers, "Because Braden scared me out of my pants!"

One night after dinner, four-year-old Carter barges into the dining room dressed as a pirate—tricorn hat, eye patch—waving a foam sword.

"Dad," he says sternly, "when I got up from the table, I didn't say, 'May I please be excused?' because I'm a pirate! And pirates have no manners!"

With a flourish of his sword, he's gone.

*December 14, 1999*

The week before Christmas. It's bedtime. The boys like to make up words and ask me to tell them what the words mean. Jackson says, "What is a Papusnookah?" I say, "A papusnooka is a small man with huge underpants." Gales of laughter. And so it goes, into the night.

My friend, director Louis J. Horvitz, is on the phone and hears the triplets talking in the background.

"Wow," he says, "The boys are talking!" Like it's breaking news.

I say, "Lou, they're not only talking. They're talking about *you*."

He loved that. He said, "Really?"

Okay, we're "helicopter parents." We admit it. We spend a lot of time with our children. We take them to school, to sporting events, birthday parties, playdates. We read to them, play with them in the backyard.

We draw pictures for them to color. We monitor their schoolwork, how much time they spend watching television and videos. We don't allow them to play video games yet. We're paying attention to their lives.

Our parents didn't pay attention to us the way parents do now. More than once, I heard my father say, "Children should be seen and not heard." Pop was busy with his career and supporting our family. He didn't have a lot of time to devote to us or our interests. More than anything, I believe it was a generational thing. My father's father was the bishop of the Episcopal Church in Oklahoma. The bishop didn't have a lot of time for his sons. He had a flock to tend to.

It takes a lot of time and money to spoil three kids at once, but we're getting it done. For example, we're actually spending time trying to come up with concepts for each of their birthday parties. Which is a little strange because a birthday party is already a concept. This year, for their fourth birthday, we're considering a train theme and having the party at Travel Town in Griffith Park on one of the old train cars.

Wait. Braden wants an "army" theme. Everyone will dress in camouflage outfits and all the presents will be guns and tanks.

I tell him, "Let's brainstorm some more ideas." They get it and take off. They propose a "live animals party" where elephants will walk through the house and flatten everybody like a pancake. When you're four, it's really funny when people get flattened like a pancake.

Then, they pitch a "car party" that will involve cars crashing through our front doors and flattening everybody like a pancake.

I pitch a "cooking party." Barbecue some chicken, make cupcakes or cookies, serve a pasta dish and a salad. Pour some wine for the adults. Doesn't involve flattening people but it could be fun. I get zero buy-in.

They suggest a "camping party"—all their friends come over and sleep in tents in the backyard. We roast marshmallows on a campfire, sing songs, and distribute poison ivy. Hold on. What about a "games" party involving hula hoops, a sack race, and playing Trouble and Checkers, their favorite board games?

Barb and I have an idea—a "tree cutting party." We have two big, dead pine trees in the backyard. A team of tree trimmers will come over and cut the trees while the kids watch and eat cake. It could work.

*Chapter 6*

# WHAT LEARNING CURVE?

> *When your children are teenagers, it's important to have a dog so that someone in the house is happy to see you.*
> —NORA EPHRON, AUTHOR AND SCREENWRITER

Disclaimer: If you're a parent reading this, or you're reading this book for advice on parenting, please keep in mind that when it comes to parenting, we're working at a considerable disadvantage. There's no learning curve for us. We're learning everything for the first time with three kids, all at once, and then it's onto the next thing. We don't have a "first child" to teach us what to do as parents. We don't have grandparents who, if you ask, will offer advice. We stumble blindly into each phase of childhood and parenting *times three*, simultaneously, hoping to get through it and get some of it right.

As a parent, you say things you never imagined would come out of your mouth:

"Don't drink out of the cat's bowl."

"Take the noose off your brother's neck."

And you answer questions you never thought you'd be asked. This morning, we're trying to explain "tomorrow" to the boys. We get through explaining it, and Carter says, "When will it be tomorrow? Is it tomorrow yet?" Uh, no. But the next day, we think they're starting to get the concept when Carter asks, "Is this tomorrow *now*?"

Tomorrow is a difficult concept even for adults. I tell Barbara, "We must think we're about to die, because we're spending money like there's no tomorrow."

The other concept that's hard to explain to four-year-olds is time: "It'll take us an hour to get there, boys."

"Is an hour a long time?" Jackson asks.

"No, well, an hour is an hour; it's twice as long as a half hour—about four times as long as it takes to get to school."

We realize this is going nowhere when Jackson asks again, "But is an hour a long time?"

We finally have to admit, "Yes. It is." When you've been alive for only thirty-five thousand hours, an hour is a long time.

It's a warm summer night. I'm standing in the doorway to the nursery. We're talking about cats and coyotes. This morning, while we were all having breakfast, we saw a coyote in our backyard running back and forth, apparently chasing one of our cats. Barbara and I ran outside screaming guttural, fear-inducing screams. The terrified coyote tore up the hill behind the house and jumped a six-foot fence with room to spare. Tonight, as sleep approaches, Jackson says quietly, "Dad, I think I heard that coyote outside tonight."

"Really?"

"Yeah. He said, 'Where's that cat?'"

The boys are falling asleep, ready to welcome unseen dreams. And I have to say, three four-year-old boys are really at their best when they're asleep. As we watch them drift off, I'm feeling grateful that we have all that matters and some of what doesn't matter. What matters is we have our health—three boys who are healthy and whole. We have a roof over our head, food in the refrigerator, a car, work, friends, family. We could use one more *parent* or some grandparents, but that's okay. We have what matters. What's silly is how much time we spend trying to get more of what doesn't matter.

Jackson is having a dream. He calls out for "Mommy" in a plaintive voice. Barbara goes to him. "Mommy, I want to be on the ladder." Barbara places a reassuring hand on his back. "Who's on the ladder?" she asks softly. Jackson, eyes closed and falling asleep, pauses as if absorbing the question then answers, "Braden." Another pause, then Barbara says softly, rubbing his back, "I know how it is when you want to be on the ladder." Jackson's in dreamland.

Carter loves his "blankie," the small, soft, blue and white woven blanket he's had since he came home from the hospital. Yes, it's the one I purchased at Toys "R" Us. He's especially fixed on the corner. The corner is symbolic. The edge of the blanket is nondescript. You don't know where you are when your fingers are moving down the edge of the blanket, but when you get to the corner, you're at the place where the sides meet. Carter is reassured when he reaches the corner. He can rest. He likes to put the corner in his mouth.

Today, I finally found a few minutes to sit down and read a book—*The Little Engine That Could*. So good.

Bedtime is always a sweet time. Our ritual is a bath, reading a story, music, then sleep. This night, the guys are in bed, ready for sleep, but Jackson wants to tell his brothers a bedtime story.

He begins, "Once upon a time there was a boy named Carter who didn't want to go to sleep. He wanted to stay up all night."

Carter's doing his best to keep his eyes open.

Jackson continues, "Then, Carter pooped in his diaper and fire came out of his butt!"

Big laugh. Even Carter's laughing. The words "poop" and "butt" are huge with four-year-olds. They don't just resonate. They dominate.

## Training Wheels

The triplets are going on five. They're attending preschool in Encino now, and they all have bicycles with training wheels. One afternoon, when they're riding around on the patio and the backyard with great enthusiasm, Carter stops and asks me to take the training wheels off his bike. I say, "No, buddy, I don't think you're ready to ride without training wheels yet," or something to that effect. Dad Think. Inner voice unspoken: *Oh boy, the time has come to teach the boys how to ride bikes. Times three. But this doesn't seem like the right time.*

Carter insists. "Please take my training wheels off."

I know if I do what he wants, I'll end up putting the trainers back on again, but he won't take no for an answer, so I give in. And the minute the training wheels are off, he's tooling around the patio and the yard with ease. I'm not following him or holding him or assisting him in any way. I'm just watching Carter ride his bike!

## WHAT LEARNING CURVE?

Wait, how is this possible? In the America I grew up in, dads taught their kids how to ride a bike by holding onto the back of the seat and running along behind them. Come to find out the preschool has a special two-wheel bicycle that the kids have been learning on. It has a large front tire and a small rear tire which allows the kids' feet to touch the ground while they're learning to balance using the large front wheel. Beautiful! They taught themselves to ride a bike, before they started kindergarten, by riding this brilliantly designed bicycle. Life is good.

Five-year-olds are great. They're potty-trained. They can dress themselves. Soon they'll be starting kindergarten. Our "babies" are not "babies" anymore, but from time to time they revert. We're finishing dinner, and the boys have been excused. We're enjoying a glass of wine, talking about the day and the food. "Boy, the spaghetti was really tasty tonight." And then you hear it from the downstairs bathroom:

"Mommy-Daddy (as if we're one person), would you please wipe my bottom?"

What? They still want us to wipe their bottoms? That'll change the bouquet on a good red wine. It's an invitation you just hate to pass up, but I notice we never volunteer for each other. You seldom hear, "I'll get it." More often, "I think it's your turn."

Riding in the car with the boys is always interesting. We're trying to be careful about what we say, including cursing at traffic or arguing with each other. But we love to hear what they say. And they say things.

Today, we're picking them up from a summer camp they're attending before they go to kindergarten. As he gets in the car, Jackson has a worried look on his face. "One of our friends said a bad word at camp today . . . it was the f-word."

We brace ourselves for a conversation we're not quite ready to have. "The f-word?"

Jackson continues. "Yeah . . . f-f-f . . . f-f-f . . . fart!"

Laughter in the back seat. Relief in the front.

Barbara: "Oh yes, that is a very bad word."

Some of our family practices—Choice Man, for example—are meant to reduce friction and create order out of chaos. Others are designed to encourage safety and keep the number of ER visits to a minimum. With three energetic boys, it's easy to see how a *Lord of the Flies* type of atmosphere could develop. A lot of the time, it feels like we're just one butterfly Band-Aid or tourniquet away from disaster.

Triplet boys definitely need regulation. Education, recreation, appreciation, and regulation. As the boys get older, we develop a set of house rules. Here's a list they created after being told a thousand times:

1. No balls in the house.
2. No falling from trees.
3. No shoving.
4. No hitting.
5. No drawing on walls.
6. No running with scissors.
7. No spitting.
8. No climbing on roof.

And, added by Braden . . .
9. No farting on Daddy.

We also have some axioms to live by: Don't hit your brother unless you're ready to get hit back. Never poke a perfect fire. Never flush another man's poo.

We're also trying to instill in them certain values and ethics. Displayed in their playroom is copy of what we're calling "The Casady Code of Ethics," which we have shamelessly borrowed from Arnold Orville Beckman, the inventor of the pH meter and founder of Beckman Instruments. It reads:

THE CASADY CODE OF ETHICS
1. Always tell the truth. Absolute integrity in everything you do.
2. Do your best at all times.
3. Never harm others.
4. Never do anything you'll be ashamed of.
5. There is no satisfactory substitute for excellence.
6. Moderation in all things, including moderation.
7. Don't take yourself too seriously.

The boys are poised to start kindergarten. One day in the car, Carter says, "Mom, in two weeks, we go to kindergarten."

Barb says, "That's right."

Carter continues. "Kindergarten, then first grade, second grade, third grade, fourth grade, fifth grade . . ." We figure he's practicing counting.

"Sixth grade, seventh grade, eighth grade, ninth grade, tenth grade, eleventh grade, twelfth grade . . . then college, job, old man, dead."

Wow. Nailed it. And he's five years old. Should we be concerned?

## Making Art

The fellas are in kindergarten. One afternoon, Jackson comes into the kitchen and asks Barbara whether he can have some paper towels and tape. She says, "Sure," and hands over the requested supplies. A short time later, Jackson reappears and says, "Look at what I made." He's holding a bird, a white dove, made of paper towels Scotch taped together; it has big wings, a sleek body, and a head with a tapered beak. It's astounding. Barbara offers him a marking pen and suggests he add eyes, which he does, expertly, with two little dots. His creation is beautiful, not to mention impressive, astonishing, and almost impossible to comprehend.

The next day, Barbara takes Jackson's dove to school and shows it to the vice principal. She's aghast. "Oh, my goodness," she stammers. "Gifted. Gifted. He's gifted."

## November 2000

Braden, Carter, and Jackson are about to turn six. And America is suddenly changing in another way we never imagined. It's election day. Former Vice President Al Gore is running for president against former Texas Governor George W. Bush. Gore wins the popular vote by more than five hundred thousand votes, but a dispute erupts over voting irregularities in Florida, including a flawed "butterfly" ballot in Miami. "W's" brother, Jeb Bush, is Florida's governor, so it looks like the fix is in for W, and, understandably, Vice President Gore is demanding a recount in Florida.

Bush sues to stop the recount called for by the Florida Supreme Court (for fear he might lose), and the case goes to the US Supreme Court. The US Supreme Court, known for its reluctance to interfere in matters that are historically left up to the states (like running elections and counting votes), steps in and makes an unprecedented ruling to stop the recount when Bush is ahead of Gore by 537 votes. Bush's victory in Florida gives him the advantage in the Electoral College and thus the presidency. In other words, by its unprecedented decision, the Supreme Court effectively awards the election to Bush and then stipulates that its decision can never be cited as precedent in the future. A study conducted a year after the election concludes that, in fact, Gore won Florida in 2000.*

We've just put the boys to bed and we're switching back and forth between Anderson Cooper on CNN and Brian Williams on NBC, trying to make sense of it all. Barbara is saying, "This is the beginning of the end."

Too dramatic? In retrospect, maybe not.

---

\* The National Opinion Research Center (NORC) at the University of Chicago, sponsored by a consortium of major United States news organizations, conducted the Florida Ballot Project to determine the reliability and accuracy of the systems used in the voting process, including how different systems correlated with voter overvotes and undervotes. The review's findings were reported in the media during the week after November 12, 2001, by the organizations that funded the recount: Associated Press, CNN, the *Wall Street Journal*, the *New York Times*, the *Washington Post*, the *St. Petersburg Times*, the *Palm Beach Post*, and Tribune Publishing, which included the *Los Angeles Times*, *South Florida Sun-Sentinel*, *Orlando Sentinel*, and the *Chicago Tribune*. Based on the NORC review, the media group concluded that if the disputes over the validity of all the ballots in question had been consistently resolved and any uniform standard applied, the electoral result would have been reversed and Gore would have won by 60 to 171 votes. An analysis of the NORC data by University of Pennsylvania researcher Steven F. Freeman and journalist Joel Bleifuss concluded that, no matter what standard is used, after a recount of all uncounted votes, Gore would have been the victor.

## *Christmas Break 2000*

We haven't taken the boys on an airplane until now. We didn't want to be those parents trying to console *three* crying babies or whining toddlers. Now that they're five-turning-six, they're old enough to sit still and amuse themselves with playing cards, coloring books, and snacks. We're flying from Los Angeles to Reno, Nevada—one hour and fifteen minutes—to introduce them to flying and skiing, at Northstar California Ski Resort near Lake Tahoe. Oh, and we haven't taken them skiing until now because they each need to be able to carry their own boots, skis, and poles. Three of them, two of us with our own boots, skis, and poles. So yeah.

We're on the mountain having a wonderful time. Barbara and I are skiing together. The triplets are in ski school. At lunch, we connect with their instructor, a tall Australian guy who eagerly gives us a spot-on report, not only about their progress on skis but also their personalities.

"Braden is quietly mastering it and doing very well," he says in his down-under accent. "Jackson is right behind, a bit more cautious and very interested in getting things just right. Carter, on the other hand, goes straight down the hill and doesn't see the need to learn to stop. And by the way, he can talk the leg off a chair, can't he?"

It's fascinating to see the individual personalities of the boys blossoming and mirroring who they seemed to be right from the start. It's also fascinating that, in one morning on the slopes, their ski instructor has the triplets fairly well figured out.

*Getaway*

We don't do it often, but if we can get "covered" and get away from the grind of coping with six-year-olds for an afternoon or a night, we try to do it. We call it "Sanity Management." Today, we're driving down the hill to the Mondrian Hotel on Sunset Boulevard, all of seven minutes from our house. When we arrive, the doorman asks, "Where are you in from?" We say, "Just up the hill." He looks at us funny as we go inside. The triplets are at home with Rosa and their Uncle Derek and Aunt Nancy. Angels all.

We call home to be polite. Carter shares that he hit his head near his eye on the doorframe and got an "owie"—not a cut, just a red bump. Then, Jackson admits he hit Carter with the little black plastic bowling ball "on accident" (as opposed to "on purpose"). Braden reports that he was skateboarding, crashed, and broke one of the terracotta pots near the place in the yard they call "Dinosaur Land." Oh, and Carter got scratched by a rosebush, no Band-Aid needed. Also, Carter reports he found a quarter and named it "Bob." Jackson and Braden report that "Carter loves an oak tree."

Good night, boys.

*Lest We Forget . . .*

First grade is scary. Not only for the triplets but also for us and for America. It's September 11, 2001. We're up early. We've got the little TV in the kitchen on while the boys eat breakfast. Suddenly, we're looking at the horrifying images. We briefly hear the breaking news and quickly turn the sound off. We don't want to alarm the boys. But we know it's bad. Do we take them to school? Is the entire country being attacked? We turn off the TV.

The boys sense the sudden change in our demeanor. "What's happening?"

We tell them we don't know. We talk to friends on the phone and decide to do what we usually do. We're going to school.

At school, the other parents are doing what they usually do, but we're all scared.

The boys, who are six, know about trains. They don't know anything about New York, trade, or the World Trade Center. As he gets out of the van, Carter asks me, "Dad, did something bad happen to the World *Train* Center?"

I say, "No, the trains are going to be okay."

We hug them a little tighter than usual and let them go.

In the America we came up in, there were some incredibly dramatic instances of commercial airliners being hijacked at gunpoint and passengers being held as hostages. But mostly the hijackers wanted money and, typically, after they were paid or captured, the hostages were let go. Hijackings are frightening, but no one I know ever imagined airplanes full of people being used as flying bombs. And yet the horror of that is exactly what we're witnessing. Two planes full of innocent people have been used to bring down the twin towers of the World Trade Center in New York; another airliner full of people has been flown into the Pentagon in Washington, DC. Brave passengers have forced a third hijacked airliner, intended for the US Capitol Building, to crash in a field outside Shanksville, Pennsylvania, killing everyone on board.

We don't know whether there are going to be similar attacks all over America. We're feeling an overwhelming sense of dread; the country we assumed was a safe place to live and raise our children suddenly seems dangerous and unsafe at every turn. America is different now. We are different now.

Eighty-two days after 9/11, on December 2, 2001, just as we're beginning to see through the fear and fog of terrorism, there's another breathtaking event. Enron, a giant Texas energy company and a darling of Wall Street, collapses and declares bankruptcy. At the time, Enron is one of the largest companies in America. Founded in 1985 by Kenneth Lay as a merger between two relatively small regional companies, Houston Natural Gas and InterNorth, Enron grew rapidly and massively based on falsified financial statements. When what turned out to be an enormous shell game collapsed, $65 billion in equity disappeared overnight and twenty-seven thousand people lost their jobs.

And that's only part of the fallout. We know about Enron because it's been interfering in how electricity is supplied to the state of California where we live, causing what we suspect is a completely artificial "energy crisis." This "crisis" will fuel the recall of then-Governor Gray Davis, a Democrat. Davis will be replaced in 2003 by Arnold Schwarzenegger, a Republican, who, most pundits agree, would not have survived a normal election cycle. But because Davis is removed midterm, Schwarzenegger benefits from a short election cycle in which his weaknesses, not to mention the numerous accusations of sexual abuse against him, received relatively little attention. (The so-called energy crisis that undid Gray Davis will prove to be as phony as Enron, and Arnold Schwarzenegger will father a child with his maid, so there was no energy shortage there either.)

The evaporation overnight of Enron's $65 billion in assets make it the largest corporate bankruptcy in US history until a company called WorldCom declares bankruptcy *the next year*. Why did Enron collapse? Or WorldCom? In a word, deregulation. What few regulators were left had placed their blind trust in the industries they regulated to conduct their businesses safely. With that as a guiding principle, what could possibly go wrong?

Stay tuned. We'll see.

*Spell, Spell, Spell*

Family dinners with first graders often involve some cajoling to get them to eat their vegetables. Especially broccoli. We keep putting it on their plates. They keep refusing to eat it. We tell them broccoli is a "little tree" and "trees are good." Finally, tonight, Jackson decides to eat his "tree." He likes it. His brothers eat their "trees." They like broccoli! Small victory with big implications.

For entertainment at dinner, I've come up with a game show called *Spell, Spell, Spell*, which I announce in the dulcet tones of a typical game show host:

"Welcome to *Spell, Spell, Spell*, the word game that tests your spelling skills while you're eating dinner. Tonight, on *Spell, Spell, Spell*, we have Braden Casady. Where are you from, Braden?"

Before Braden can answer, I say, "Sorry, we're out of time, because it's time right now to play *Spell, Spell, Spell*." They laugh. I continue: "If you get the word right, you win nothing, and if you get the word wrong, we slap you with a fly swatter and catapult you into the neighbor's yard!" More laughter. We then proceed to play a legitimate spelling game. They're learning the definitions and how to spell words like "geography" and "persistence" as well as unusual ones like "ubiquitous" and "onomatopoeia," which they are intrigued to learn are words made from the sound associated with that word, (i.e., cuckoo, sizzle, buzz). They like onomatopoeia. Dissolve. One day after school, the boys' first grade teacher tells Barbara that she asked the kids whether they could think of another word for "small." All three of our kids raised their hands and, one after the other, blurted out: "Weensy." "Microscopic." "Minuscule!"

Their teacher was amazed. The word she was looking for was "little." Small game with big implications?

## *"Take a Break!"*

When the boys are six-turning-seven, we notice that they don't just *watch* television, they *replicate* it. After they watch basketball, they go outside and imitate the moves of professional players. They watch baseball and reenact the way the guys in the Big Leagues play, their stance, the way they hold their bats. As a TV producer, I'm fascinated by this, and worried. It's not a bad thing. Until it is.

They love to watch World Wrestling Entertainment (WWE); they're fans of Rey Mysterio and John Cena, and they're starting to wrestle with each other.

At one point, one of the boys throws his brother to the playroom floor and threatens to hit him with a wooden chair. I quickly intervene to explain that the most important letter in WWE is the "E" which stands for "entertainment." They look at me funny. I explain that the wrestlers on WWE are performers, that they have routines they rehearse before they fight, that the ring is specially padded and outfitted with springs to cushion their falls.

"Guys, this is entertainment. Trust me. Your dad knows something about entertainment. You've heard of 'the entertainment business?' That's the business I'm in . . ."

They start to listen.

The boys still sleep in the same room, but the cribs that turned into daybeds have been replaced by three twin beds. The guys have pushed their beds together to make their own padded "ring." Jackson has made a "chair"—a flat, chair-shaped thing—out of cardboard and duct tape, that's flexible so you can hit a guy with it and not kill him.

One minute they're watching WWE on TV, and the next they're on the beds imitating what they've seen. They go at it, full-on. Jumping, tumbling, wrestling each other to the "mat," pinning each other down, hitting each other with the "chair." It's intense.

I monitor the action periodically with one simple goal in mind: avoid a trip to the emergency room. They could fly into the windows or the dresser if it gets too crazy.

At some point, I know I'm going in.

But I don't tell them to "Stop!" Because rambunctious boys don't like to be told to "Stop!" especially in the middle of a heated "competition." I'm not sure how I know this—maybe it's a guy thing—but I decide to tell them to take a break. That's it!

So, just when it feels like there could be an ER visit in our future, I step into the room and say, not as a parent but as if I'm their coach, "Okay, guys, take a break!" And the most amazing thing happens. They say "Okay," hop off the beds and head downstairs to cool off, get a snack, and relax for a while.

### Second Grade

The boys' second grade teacher uses a behavior chart to keep the kids in line. Our boys are all in the same class because we want them to be together. There is a school of thought among parents of multiples that it's a good idea to split them up. But our triplets are fraternal, not identical; they're unique, social, and capable of distinguishing themselves without being separated. Plus, keeping them together—this is second grade, after all—may provide them with a modicum of comfort and security.

One morning at breakfast, Braden explains the behavior chart. The teacher has a warning system: Green = good behavior. Pink = Warning. Yellow = twenty minutes in the back of the class. Blue = call the parents. Red = go to the principal's office.

Braden reports he's got "greens" (good boy) and one pink. Jackson also has greens and two pinks. Carter pauses: "I've got pinks, and I'm in the yellows."

We're not worried. Carter's chatty. Maybe a little too chatty in class?
Barbara asks: "What do you like most about your teacher?"
Braden says, "She's effective."
Jackson: "Her nipples. I mean her dimples."
Gales of laughter. Carter's laughing so hard he can't speak.

Before they go to school, the boys like to roughhouse and blow off steam in the backyard. We think it's a good idea for them to expend some of their boundless energy before they have to sit still in a classroom. This morning, they're having a pillow fight in the playroom. Jackson takes the large seat cushion from the sofa, wallops Braden with it, and Braden collapses. Jackson says: "See? Size does matter."

*Chapter 7*

# THREE TO GET READY

> *Encourage and support your kids because children are apt to live up to what you believe of them.*
> —LADY BIRD JOHNSON, FORMER FIRST LADY OF THE UNITED STATES

I wish my mom could see our three boys. She would have loved them, having raised five of her own. When we were growing up, my brothers and I liked to make our mother laugh. I think we felt if we could do that, it would help alleviate some of the stress of raising the five of us. And when we did something that made her laugh, my oldest brother, Derek, would always say in a sardonic voice, "Keep laughing, Mama!" as if to say, "You're laughing now, but just wait." And that would make her laugh even harder.

*Sometime in 2002*

The guys are seven, and Lanai Road Elementary School is on its way to becoming an outstanding public school again. Barbara Casady is PTA president. Our kids are in second grade, and we're clear: some things in life are incomprehensible. This was true in my father's America. It was true in the America my brothers and I grew up in and, apparently, it's true in the America we're leaving to our three boys. There are mysteries that just can't be unraveled.

One of them is *the peach in the dryer.*

While I'm emptying the clothes dryer, I see this yellowish, sticky goo all over the inside of the dryer. As I remove the clothes and wipe the goo off the dryer drum with a damp cloth, I noticed it smells like a peach. And then I find it. A peach pit. In the dryer. But how?

I ask the boys whether they know anything about it. It's kind of hard to address.

"Hey, guys, did you put a peach in the dryer?"

They're saying, "No," and going back to what they're doing.

"Is anybody missing a peach?" I ask.

Nobody is. Barbara and I are trying our best to imagine what possibly could have happened. We imagine, for example, that someone in the family—neither of us, by the way—has put a pair of pants or shorts in the laundry and absent mindedly left a peach in the pocket. Who does that? Could that happen? When we or the nanny put clothes in the washer or dryer, we usually check the pockets for peaches.

Okay, let's say the peach goes undetected into the washer. Could happen.

Small peach. Big pocket. Lots of other laundry. Wouldn't the peach dissolve in the wash cycle? You might find a peach *pit* in a pocket when the clothes are moved to the dryer, but a whole peach sufficient to leave a dryer full of goo?

Or wait, what about this? While the dryer was running, maybe someone just chucked a perfectly good peach into the dryer to dry it off or add flavor to the load. We don't know. And apparently, we're never going to find out. The peach in the dryer remains one of those unknowable mysteries to this day.

Note to Braden, Carter, and Jackson: If either of you is able to clear up this mystery all these years later, no harm, no foul. We'll be relieved and celebrate with a peach pie.

One morning at the breakfast table before school. Braden says, "Jackson, say something funny."

Jackson replies instantly. "Fluffer's on the loose."

We don't know who "Fluffer" is or how Jackson comes up with these things, but we're still laughing as we pile into the van and head for school.

Riding home after a baseball game. The boys are hungry and want to drive through McDonald's. We seldom go to fast-food restaurants. In fact, we tell the boys, "We don't like fast food. We like *slow* food." But today, we're stopping for a snack—French fries and drinks. The boys each get large straws for their drink cups. In the van, after they finish, they set aside the empty cups and proceed to stuff the straws into their arm pits. Not sure where they learned this. By blowing air through the straw into their arm pits, they produce the loudest, most realistic flatulence sounds we've ever heard. The first one is hilarious. Then they get better and funnier. The car is swaying with laughter. I'm hoping we don't get pulled over.

The boys are old enough to do chores to earn their allowance: make their beds, clear their dishes from the table, dig a little bit on the *pool* every day.

I love that joke. We don't have a pool. Yet.

Having three boys the same age is like having three Underwriters Laboratory (UL) toy testers in your home. They stress-test every toy the moment they get their hands on it. The amount of breakage is phenomenal. We have a hot glue gun plugged in at all times. And we've shamelessly adopted comedian Jeff Foxworthy's line: "If it ain't broke, it ain't ours."

*June 2002*

Right after school lets out, we fly to Maui, where Barbara and I honeymooned as a young, footloose and fancy-free couple. Twenty years later, with kids, we're staying in a two-bedroom condo at Wailea Elua Village next to the beach. There's a pool, paddle tennis courts, lovely paths for walking, and the ocean is gentle and welcoming.

The first time we came here, the boys were five, and Barbara's generous sister, Marsha, was here to help—not this time. We're cooking three meals a day, supervising trips to the pool, ocean, and paddle tennis court, arranging games on the lawn, taking hikes, and cleaning up after the boys. We're on duty. Morning, noon, and night.

At the end of the week, we're flying home. We're seated in a row with five seats in the middle of the plane. Barbara's on one end; I'm on the other end; the triplets are in between us. They've had a great week. I pulled them into the waves on a blow-up raft; they loved that. They jumped into our arms from the side of the pool. We played paddle tennis—their hand-eye coordination is impressive. We played catch on the lawn, ran on the beach, explored a luau next door.

And now, heading home, we're exhausted. They're asleep. And in my airplane-induced stupor, I look at Barb, across the chests of our three sleeping boys. She leans forward, looking similarly exhausted, as if she's seeing me for the first time, and says, "Oh, hi! Are you working this trip?"

*August 2002*

Late summer, after Hawaii. Thank goodness Barbara graduated from UCLA because, as a Bruin, she's entitled to attend Bruin Woods, the university's world-class family camp on Lake Arrowhead, about two hours from Los Angeles. We've been coming to Bruin Woods since the boys were five. The place is idyllic with a gigantic green lawn, tennis courts, and a sand volleyball court with Lake Arrowhead just beyond. It has everything for everyone—kids and parents of all ages. The place is like Club Med done right.

From the moment we arrive and settle into our condo, our kids are cared for by brilliant UCLA students who serve as counselors, coaches, and caretakers, while we enjoy reading, napping, swimming, playing tennis, and the honor bar where you pay a modest flat fee for an entire week of drinking. We eat breakfast, lunch, and dinner together as a family in the resort's fabulous restaurant or on the spacious patio. And we tuck the boys into bed at night. Bottom line: This is a family vacation you don't want to end.

Not long after we left this serene place last summer, the horror of 9/11 happened. Now, watching the boys play on the lawn, it feels safe, surreal, even though we now know the world outside of here is much more dangerous than we thought it was a year ago.

*October 2004*

The elementary school years are flying by. The triplets are nine years old, and in June 2006, they'll graduate from fifth grade at Lanai Road Elementary. Jackson is president of their class. In anticipation of the next stage in their schooling, for the past several years, we've been investigating area middle schools and high schools in Agoura, Calabasas, Thousand Oaks, Beverly Hills, La Cañada, Pasadena, Cerritos, and Manhattan Beach.

We've always wanted to live by the ocean, and Manhattan Beach has its own school district with a California Distinguished, National Blue Ribbon middle school and an outstanding high school, Mira Costa. We're sold on the schools, so we buy a house in East Manhattan Beach located between the middle school and the high school. Until our boys finish elementary school in Encino, we rent it to a lovely family that's building a new house closer to the beach.

## Our Favorite Pastime

After many afternoons practicing in the backyard, we took the boys to play T-ball at Encino Little League, a sublime baseball oasis near us. They were five. In T-ball, after the kids hit the ball off a tee, they often act out their understanding of the game of baseball in hilarious ways. One boy, after smacking the ball into the outfield, runs straight out to the chain link fence in the outfield, touches it, and runs triumphantly back to home plate. Another time, two five-year-olds in the outfield start to go after a ball but get distracted by a large butterfly and start chasing it instead.

The triplets continue playing baseball at Encino Little League and benefiting from some great coaching. My role is clear: I'm a fan. I want to be able to say, "One of the best things *I never did* was coach my sons in baseball." No offense to dads or moms who coach their sons or daughters, but from what I've seen, the kids often do better with "neutral" or "outside" coaches. Our guys are beginning to concentrate on certain positions on the team. Jackson is usually in center field. Braden is in the infield, usually at shortstop or second base. Carter plays first and third, but he also pitches.

Still, for all the baseball in their lives, the guys haven't been to a major league ballpark yet. So we enter a lottery at their elementary school for a chance to buy five-dollar tickets to a Dodgers game. And we win! We buy five tickets and set out for Dodger Stadium.

Before we go, I get some advice from my friend, Mike Polito, a Dodgers fan and one of the best video editors in Hollywood. He warns me, "Their first game? Oh man, the boys are gonna want to eat everything in sight . . . hot dogs, peanuts, popcorn, soft drinks, ice cream. Don't let 'em or you'll be sorry," he says. "They'll be throwing up all over the place." Duly noted. We ordered one Dodger Dog and a small drink for each. Thanks, Mike.

Our five seats in the outfield pavilion are as far from home base as you can get and still be in the stadium. We're at least 395 feet from the batter. No problem. It's a beautiful day. We're at a major league baseball game. The stadium is beautiful, the game is on, the boys are thrilled, and they have their gloves. It could happen.

"Mom . . . Dad," Carter exclaims, "these are the best seats ever!"

"Yes, they are."

The boys have played successfully on many teams at Encino Little League, which, we're now told, is instituting tryouts and a draft system. The president of Encino Little League is telling Barbara that our kids may end up on three different teams.

"Craig," Barbara tells the president, "our boys are all going to be on the same team."

"But Barbara," Craig says, "I don't think you understand. At this age, there are tryouts and a draft."

"I understand, Craig," Barb says firmly, "and our boys are going to be on the same team. We're not going to three different practices and three different games to see our boys play just because the league thinks it's a good idea. We also don't want to encourage any more competition between them than already exists," she adds. "Do you have any idea what it's like raising triplet two-year-olds? This is payback time."

The Casady Brothers play on the same team for the rest of their time at Encino Little League. When the coaches pick one Casady boy, they burn three draft rounds, but they're happy to do it because all three are talented, coachable players, and the other parents and players like it because the teams are competitive and a lot of fun.

### Arts and Crafts

From the beginning, the triplets have had a playroom in our house that's dedicated to them. They're not allowed to play in living room, dining room, our office, the guest room, or our bedroom unless we're with them. Those are "adult areas." (As they get older, we let them help make a fire in the living room fireplace, with supervision. There were a couple of winters in Encino when I think we had a fire in the fireplace every day.) The guys' playroom has shelves, drawers, and cubicles for their toys and games, a table, a sofa called "Cricket the Couch," a TV and VCR, and three little armchairs for watching videos. It's a toddler cave, a preschooler's paradise, a grade schooler's game room. Their domain.

One afternoon after school, Jackson asks whether he can rummage through the "junk drawer" in the kitchen. The guys are ten, so we let him. He comes away with several empty split round metal key rings of various sizes. Now, he wants a pair of pliers. That's cool. We give him a pair of needle-nose pliers. Jackson has a history of making things. Remember the dove?

The next thing we know, Jackson has opened one of the metal key rings with the pliers, wrapped it around a beautiful marble from their trove, and attached the "imprisoned stone" to a chain to make a necklace. Before long, all three boys are at the table in their playroom making necklaces out of key rings and marbles. They ask us to please get them more key rings and chains; they have plenty of marbles. For the next several days, a veritable jeweler's bench is in full operation. Including the day when Max Goen, one of their friends from Encino Little League, comes over for a playdate. Later, when Max's father, Bob, a good friend, asks Max,

"What did you do at the Casadys today?" And Max says, "We made jewelry." Bob's kind of worried.

The creations are beautiful. Who knew grade schoolboys could make jewelry *and* play baseball? (Most of the necklaces were given as gifts, but Barbara still wears a couple of them to this day and always gets compliments.)

*October 2005*

We figure it's never too early to teach young boys good manners. God knows we've been trying. At the suggestion of a neighbor with a boy the same age as our guys, we've enrolled the triplets in a cotillion class. The main purpose of a cotillion, as you know if you grew up in eighteenth-century Europe and America, is to "teach respectful manners to young people so they can go out into society and thrive." At least that's what the brochure says. Typically offered to kids in fourth grade through eighth grade, cotillion classes teach boys how to introduce themselves, shake hands—a firm grip with eye contact—ask a young lady to dance, dance politely, and generally behave in a social setting. Our guys are fifth graders—ten going on eleven—and this feels like a good time to introduce them to civilized behavior. To attend, they must wear suits, ties, and dress shoes. Three words come to mind: Burlington Coat Factory. The suits, dress shirts, and ties are reasonable. The shoes are twelve dollars a pair, also reasonable given they will outgrow them in a year.

As we pile out of the van and enter the cotillion at the Woodland Hills Country Club, the boys look spectacular, like they just stepped out of an ad for the Burlington Coat Factory. Their training begins at the door, where each boy learns to introduce himself to one of the matrons in proper fashion. Once inside, they are seated with a bunch of well-suited boys their age across the dance floor from a bunch of girls their age in fancy dresses. It's incredibly charming and civilized. As the evening progresses, they learn how to politely ask a young lady to dance, how to dance respectfully, how to properly bring their partners refreshments, and, at the end of the evening, how to politely say "good night." On the way home, the boys say they had a good time, but maybe they're just being polite.

*June 2006*

The elementary school years have vanished in a cool summer breeze. By the time our boys leave fifth grade, Barbara Casady, mother of triplets, has served as president of the Lanai Road School PTA and on the board of the 501(c)(3) nonprofit foundation, Friends of Lanai, for three and a half years running. Throughout the process of producing and participating in Halloween carnivals, student fairs, pledge drives, phone banks, comedy nights, and every other conceivable fundraising and fun-raising event we could think of, we're glad we took the ten-year deduction. We're managing to look the part and, so far, our kids, their friends, many of our friends, and most of the parents at the school are none the wiser.

More importantly, we feel grateful to be part of a group that's made such a remarkable difference at our local school. The level of parent participation and the extent of the transformation is truly extraordinary and genuinely moving. Before we finally wave goodbye to Lanai Road Elementary, LAUSD officials, aware of the school's remarkable metamorphosis, ask to meet with the board members and key supporters of Friends of Lanai. They want to know what the parents did to turn the school around. Tears come to the eyes of everyone in the group as they admit, "We did everything."

By being a "squeaky wheel" with the school district and the school board, raising money and awareness, Lanai Road School got a talented new principal, an added position for a vice principal, a new library, a computer lab, a new playground structure thanks to Anne and Kirk Douglas, a full-time nurse, a music program, a Special Advanced Studies (SAS) program, an after-school enrichment program, encouragement, support, and recognition days for the teachers, and the entire school was painted and relandscaped. Parent tip: If your local school is on its knees, try organizing or joining a group of parents to turn it around. It can be done; it's fun, and it's incredibly rewarding. Taking the ten-year deduction is optional.

*September 4, 2006*

Before we know it, it's time to move from Encino. And it's brutal. The rafters in the garage hold things we haven't looked at since we moved in nine years ago. There seem to be countless boxes of mostly broken toys. Plus bicycles, scooters, roller skates. There's a rowing machine I haven't used for years because I've been lifting instead—babies, toddlers, preschoolers, and elementary school kids. There are file cabinets full of old business records, boxes of things we didn't want the guys to get into, Halloween and Christmas decorations.

We've been filling up our trash cans for weeks. The boys don't yell, "Trash truck, trash truck!" anymore and race out the front door to watch the cans get dumped. They have been watching us fill a rented dumpster that will soon be hauled away. Everything we want to keep, or at least everything we're keeping, is being loaded onto a truck and taken to a storage facility because we can't move into our Manhattan Beach house yet. Wait, what? The house is being renovated, so for the next few months, our temporary home will be the Marriott Residence Inn. (We end up living there for ninety days, which, by the way, is how you become a Marriott *platinum* member.)

The Manhattan Beach house is an interesting and somewhat unusual "upside-down house," meaning the kitchen, dining room, and living room are upstairs, and the bedrooms are downstairs. Upstairs, it has a southern view toward the Palos Verdes Peninsula. Downstairs, there are three equal-size bedrooms off a hall, perfect for our three guys. Barbara is completely redesigning the living room, dining room and kitchen—the heart of the house—working her architectural and artistic magic to make it gorgeous, functional, and the perfect next home for our family.

As the movers finish loading the truck, the boys and I pile into my sedan and head for the beach, expecting Barbara to follow in the minivan, which is filled with clothes and other essentials, including the fish tank with fish in it.

Barbara watches us drive away and waits for the moving van to leave. At that point she realizes she doesn't have her car keys. She calls the movers, figuring they've picked up her keys, but there's no answer. Panic. Finally, Barb reaches the owner on his cell; he calls the moving crew, and the truck comes back. The movers have scooped up Barb's car keys along with the last piece of furniture taken from the entry of the house.

*September 5, 2006*

Tuesday morning after Labor Day, our family is waking up in Manhattan Beach for the first time, after spending our first night at the Residence Inn. It's the first day of middle school. Yep. And after taking advantage of the complimentary breakfast that includes the reason you stay at a Residence Inn—waffles—we're driving to school.

It's quiet in the car until Jackson says, "Dad?"

"Yeah?"

"You know, it would have been nice if we could have lived in Manhattan Beach for a week or two before starting middle school."

Silence.

In the rearview mirror, I can see the brothers nodding in agreement.

"Point taken," I say. "In a perfect world..."

Barbara and I are feeling understandably chastised and more than a little embarrassed.

Jackson's right. We brought the boys down to surf camp during the summer. That was good. They've been to one birthday party in Manhattan Beach with a friend they met at UCLA Family Camp. That was helpful. The middle school required them to take a math test before entering sixth grade, so they've been to the campus once. Thanks to the quality of teaching at Lanai Road Elementary, they all ranked a full year ahead in math. That was impressive. But Jackson's right.

We pull into the drop-off at Manhattan Beach Middle School. Braden, Carter, and Jackson pile out of the van, pull on their backpacks, and walk off together. It's a scene I'll never forget—our three boys in T-shirts, shorts, and Vans, walking side by side into the first day of sixth grade.

I'm thinking, *Well, at least they're not alone. They each have two friends.*

*November 2006*

It's almost Thanksgiving when we move into the Manhattan Beach house. Several things still need to be done, but most everything works. The only TV we have is a little portable one with an enormously long cable attached. We put the TV on a cart with wheels so we can roll it into the kitchen, living room, or dining room.

We're down to one cat—Lucy, the white one who adopted us and the triplets when we lived in Laurel Canyon. She's been living at the Residence Inn with us. Lucy's older now, and there's a feeling in the house, although not in me personally, that Lucy could use a companion. One day, a friend in the San Fernando Valley calls to say that a feral cat has given birth to a litter of kittens in her backyard. Would our boys want one? Barbara thinks we should get two kittens so they can keep each other company and drives the kids up to see them.

At the friend's house, there are *three* kittens corralled in the family room. Each boy promptly picks up a kitten—Braden, the fuzzy black one; Carter, the tiger stripped one; and Jackson, the black shorthair with a white chest and white paws. They immediately start bonding with their respective choices.

After a few minutes, Barbara tells our friend that we'll take two of the kittens, to which Braden says, "No, Mom. We need to take all three. They're triplets, and we're triplets."

That's why we now have four cats.

*Fall 2007*

As the boys navigate middle school, they share one cell phone; they have friends we don't know; we live in a town we don't know that well. The internet isn't just a thing—it's *everything*. And everyone is on the phone all the time—surfing "the net," texting, emailing, sometimes even talking to another human—or sharing on Facebook. We're not on Facebook yet, but I'm reading in the *LA Times* on October 24, 2007, that Microsoft is purchasing a 1.6 percent share of Facebook for $240 million, giving Facebook "a total implied value of around $15 billion." Wow. I guess we need to check out Facebook.

In my father's America, people "shared" by writing letters by hand, and some, like my dad, used a typewriter. Indeed, in the America I grew up in, before computers, the typewriter was the "word processor" of choice. Especially because I grew up in a newspaper family, I learned how to type at an early age. I aced every typing test I ever took. In high school, I remember falling asleep at night to the sound of my father typing in his office outside my bedroom. He wrote an amusing front-page column called "Along Main Street" and two hard-hitting editorials for the newspaper every day, often drafting them at night after he and my mother had come home from some community or social engagement.

In the morning when I went to school, Pop's "copy" would be hanging on a hook outside the back door waiting for a copyboy from the paper to pick it up.

I took a typewriter to college and worked on one for years until I became an early adopter of the personal computer in 1983. In college, I wrote letters home rather than make long distance phone calls, which were expensive at the time. In 1964, I sent a typewritten letter to President Lyndon Johnson congratulating him on his election. He replied with a letter typed on White House stationery. I still have the framed letter.

When the triplets were four or five, we still had a "dial-up" internet connection. Remember dial-up? That was where your internet connection was made over a telephone line, and it made a kind of high-pitched grinding sound. Now that the kids are twelve, the internet is also becoming the source of what passes for "news" but does not respect the precepts of journalism. My father and a generation of newspaper men and women like him, including those who founded and inhabited television newsrooms for the medium's first three decades, practiced the time-honored protocols of journalism. They adhered to the rule that the facts in every news story need verification from multiple credible sources. Pop and his generation, like most talented, young reporters today, practiced the kind of journalism that can protect and save a democracy. Now, even with supervised access to our computers, strangers can invade our children's lives, and they can peek into other people's lives. Despite all the technology meant to serve us, we're feeling exposed and exploited.

As we learn more about newly minted Facebook billionaire Mark Zuckerberg, we suspect he has created an enterprise that is more interested in selling data purloined from its users than connecting the world in a constructive way. Neither Zuckerberg nor Facebook is who they would like us to think they are. To make the first version of "The Facebook," Zuckerberg appropriated student photos at Harvard even after being told not to and being reprimanded by an investigative committee for doing so. He ousted the Winklevoss twins, who originated the idea for the enterprise and allegedly cheated his other remaining partner out of ownership and control. Facebook fails to protect user data and vacillates about posting false information on the site, justifying it all in the name of "free speech" while making a profit for himself and his shareholders. Private profit over public good. Is that good business, good citizenship, or just another example of greed?

(Years later, the truth about social media will be revealed in the 2019 Netflix documentary, *The Great Hack*, a must-see film for anyone with a smartphone or a computer who plans to continue living in twenty-first-century America. As Emily Dreyfuss wrote in *Wired*, "*The Great Hack* is a modern horror story. The villain is Cambridge Analytica, yes, but also Facebook, and all the systems that let people become manipulated by the digital psychological clues they leave through their lives. It's terrifying because it's true.")

Before Facebook and other tentacles of social media, it used to be said, and it used to be true: "You can have your own opinion, but you can't have your own *facts*." That's no longer true. The internet and social media allow disrupters and deceivers to distort what once were accepted facts, disseminate unsubstantiated "fake news," and propagate whatever false information suits their particular purpose or point of view.

It's time to regulate the internet and the social media giants. And not a click too soon.

## *July 2007 - Cooperstown*

In early spring, even though we're now living in Manhattan Beach, our friend, Craig, the baseball coach from Encino, calls to ask whether our boys want to go to Cooperstown Dreams Park in Upstate New York with the Encino Vipers. Located about twenty minutes from the National

Baseball Hall of Fame and Museum, the Dreams Park is a baseball mecca for twelve-year-olds. You can't go as an individual player. You can only go with a team that has a spot that is either grandfathered in or won in a lottery. The tournaments run for a week at a time between early June and mid-August. The Encino Vipers have been going to Cooperstown every summer for several years. Having played in Encino since they were five, the Casady Brothers are well known there, and Coach Craig says if he can say the Casady Brothers are going, it'll be easier to put a team together. Plus, he gets three players with one call. It's a thoughtful invitation for a unique opportunity. The boys say "yes."

Situated in what were once verdant hayfields and overhung most mornings by a gentle layer of fog, the park's twenty-two baseball fields create a dreamy baseball world like no other. The players live with their coaches in barracks at the park. Parents stay in nearby motels, bed-and-breakfasts, or rented houses. One morning, as we arrive at the park, the scene was so picturesque—shafts of sunlight piercing the fog and illuminating the fields—we feel like we've died and gone to Baseball Heaven. That's certainly what this place is for our boys.

One of the traditions at the Dreams Park is for players to trade pins with other players during the week. This involves purchasing, in advance, about one hundred pins emblazoned with the name of your team. During the week, players trade their team pin for team pins from other players, hoping to leave with a complete set representing all the teams they faced. Coach Craig suggests we purchase a set of one hundred pins for each of our kids. After I explain that I'm not about to buy three hundred Viper pins and our boys will be happy to share the trading tradition with one set of pins, he agrees that one set should be enough. The boys thought the whole pin trading experience was really cool and came back with almost a complete set. (We still have the pins they collected somewhere in a storage locker.)

For a lot of twelve-year-olds, Cooperstown Dreams Park is the last time they'll play competitive baseball. By the time most boys and girls get to seventh grade, they're finished with the game. It's not a bad thing; it's a normal thing. Our guys want to play baseball in high school and possibly college, and they're definitely distinguishing themselves as individuals in the game. Whether he's on the mound pitching or in the infield, Carter is disciplined and focused. He anticipates and activates. At bat, Jackson is "clutch," which means he stays calm, connects with the ball, and gets on base. In the outfield, he's great at reading the ball early. If it's in the air, he'll catch it. If the ball drops, he's on it. Jackson's strong and can make the throw from center field to home with one hop to the catcher. Braden, who's usually at second base or shortstop, is a combination of calm and determined. He's got no "off switch." He wants the ball. If you're playing basketball, he will steal the ball from you. In soccer, he will kick it away. In baseball, Braden will leap into the air or lay out to get the ball. Between games, Coach Craig pays our guys a big compliment. He says whenever he and the other coaches need a player and look around the dugout for who to put in, "The Casady boys are always ready."

A little dad braggin' here, but the Casady Brothers are proving to be valuable assets to the Encino Vipers. In one game, Braden makes an airborne diving catch at second base to turn a game-ending double play. Calm and determined. In another game, Jackson hits a grand slam, which is a home run with bases loaded, in case you don't know America's favorite pastime. That's "clutch." A lot of batters freeze up when faced with bases loaded; Jackson comes through.

On this day, the Vipers are in the field and our pitcher, who's been doing a great job, is getting tired. It's the final inning. There are runners on first and second and no outs. This is not good. One good hit and the other team could go up by two. A home run would put 'em up by three.

Carter is playing shortstop. Jackson is in center field. The coach decides to change the pitcher, looks around the dugout, sees Braden, and sends him in. As a parent, I don't love it when the coach puts one of my boys on the mound in a *pinch*, under pressure. Thank you very much.

His first pitch, Braden throws a ball. Tension mounts. Second pitch, Braden throws a strike, which the batter crushes. A line drive up the middle. Carter catches it in the air. Out number one. The other team has decided to try to steal second and third—a "double steal"—so the runner on second has a big lead off on his way to third and he can't get back to second. Carter steps on second base. That's out number two. The runner from first who's trying to steal second is practically at Carter. Carter lunges and tags him. Out number three. Coaches, parents, and players are all looking at each other. What the hell just happened? What happened is an unassisted triple play by Carter Casady to end the game. Disciplined and focused. And one for the books in Cooperstown.

*Chapter 8*

# TEENAGERS

*In baseball, as in life, all the important things happen at home.*
—ANONYMOUS

The boys have just turned thirteen. We've been in Manhattan Beach for about year and a half. We're flying to Des Moines, Iowa. My father was born in Des Moines, but this has nothing to do with him. We're going for two reasons: (1) to celebrate our twenty-fifth wedding anniversary. I know. We considered London, Paris, Maui, and Tahiti. But we've decided on Des Moines because (2) we're going to campaign for US Senator John Edwards for president. Wait, don't judge.

We met Edwards through our dear friends Suzelle Smith and Don Howarth and campaigned for him in 2004. We liked him. We liked that he was talking about the fact that there are two Americas—one for the rich and powerful, and one for the rest of us. Edwards was on the ticket with John Kerry in 2004, and we thought they should've won. So when we learned Edwards was running again in 2008, we signed on again. In high school, the boys have been studying history and taking Model UN, a program that trains them in critical thinking, debate, and public speaking. This will be an unusual family experience and a front row seat in "retail" presidential politics where candidates speak directly to as many voters as possible.

*January 2008*

For our twenty-fifth anniversary dinner, we take the boys to one of Des Moines's more famous restaurants and political watering holes, 801 Chophouse. We get a small private room and are joined by our dear friends, Deborah May and George DelHoyo, also in town to campaign for Edwards. We have a wonderful meal. On our way out, we pass a table where Democratic party consultants Paul Begala and James Carville are eating and drinking. The adults are excited; the kids couldn't care less.

The next few days, using the dashboard-mounted GPS navigation system in our rental car, we drive around Des Moines and Perry, knocking on doors and handing out "Edwards for President" campaign literature. The boys are game and good at "door knocking." We've never been actively involved in a presidential campaign on the ground before, certainly not as a family, and certainly not in weather as cold as Iowa is in January.

To give us an idea how often the candidates themselves have been in contact with Iowa voters, we're told to never say we know John Edwards (we do). "Chances are," we're warned, "the voter you're talking to has met John more times and knows him better than you do."

Before long, the boys ask, "When are we going tubing?" They've knocked on enough doors and seen a snow park they want to visit.

We slip out of campaign mode for a few hours to visit the Sleepy Hollow Sports Park, where tubing is all the rage. The boys have a blast. We've never been colder, including while skiing in Winter Park, Colorado, in minus-eight-degree weather. Iowans deserve a lot of credit for a lot of things, and putting up with weather this cold is surely one of them.

## TEENAGERS

One day, we're out knocking on doors and leaving literature when I get a call from a friend of my sister-in-law, Nancy. Nancy's friend lives in Ames, Iowa, where Iowa State University is located. After we figure out who each other is and exchange pleasantries, Nancy's friend says, "They're coming back!"

"Who's coming back?" I ask.

"The students," she says. "They're coming back early from winter break to campaign for Barack Obama!"

"Oh," I say, realizing we haven't been paying any attention to the Obama campaign. The Edwards campaign is entirely focused on Hillary Clinton.

The next day, we're working the phones, calling voters from a union hall. At one point, I'm surprised when Elizabeth Edwards appears behind me, puts her hand on my shoulder, and says, "Hi, Cort. Thanks for doing this."

All this activity—by the Hillary Clinton, Barack Obama, and John Edwards campaigns—is leading up to the Iowa Caucuses. Like most people, we've heard about the caucuses, but we have no real idea what they are or how they work until, one day, we're invited to be trained as precinct captains for the Edwards campaign on caucus night.

At an early-morning session in one of the breakout rooms at the hotel, we're told we're being made precinct captains for Edwards because the campaign has just learned that the Iowans who were originally assigned to be captains in a particular precinct can't make it. After being trained in caucus fundamentals by Edwards staffers, we're assigned to Waukee, a precinct in a fast-growing suburb west of Des Moines.

On caucus night, we arrive at Waukee Christian Church a few minutes before 6:00 p.m. with our supplies—stickers, signs, masking tape, cookies, sodas, the triplets, and a calculator to do the all-important math. Inside, we find the Hillary and Obama captains already hanging signs for their candidates. More disturbingly, the counter in the church kitchen is covered with a dozen boxes of cookies decorated with "Hillary" written in icing. I'm shocked. We've been told that snacks are important at a caucus, and obviously, Hillary's going to win the cookie vote hands down.

The way the caucuses work is that folks living in a given precinct report to a specified location—a home, gymnasium, meeting hall or, in our case, a church—on caucus night. They can register to vote on the spot (Republicans and Independents are allowed to register as Democrats), and then they sign in. Doors are supposed to close promptly at 7:00 p.m. Participants divide into groups based on the candidate they support. A candidate must attract at least 15 percent of the total number of caucus-goers at the location in order for that candidate to be "viable." Supporters of "nonviable" candidates are free to join another candidate or leave.

The purpose of each caucus is to elect a pre-determined number of delegates—in our case, five—to be divided among the candidates according to a mathematical formula.

Based on this precinct's numbers in 2004, we're told to expect 79 participants. By the time the chairperson closes the doors to the church at well after 7:00 p.m., there are 386 Democrats inside—a 400 percent increase that is overwhelming the process and everyone involved. While I'm gathering Edwards supporters in the multipurpose room of the church—Hillary supporters have one side of the chapel and Obama supporters the other side—and the boys are putting up posters, Barbara is helping set up and run an additional registration table. Caucus history is being made, and we are instantly part of it. The triplets are excited, taking it all in and eager to help.

The boys report that there's a long line outside the church waiting to get in. We dispatch them to work the line, passing out Edwards buttons and flyers. Braden returns after a few minutes to report, "Dad, we need more buttons! There are a lot of Edwards supporters out there." Carter adds, "There are also a lot of Obama supporters. A lot!"

With 386 participants at the caucus, the viability threshold is 58. Time to count our group. We learn that the best way to count a group of strangers is for the group to count itself. I ask each person in the gathering to simply call out their number, beginning with someone who says, "One," the next person says, "Two," and before long you get to the last person in the group who says whatever their number is, and now you know precisely how many people are in the group.

We count 92 folks for Edwards, so he's viable and entitled to one delegate; Hillary counts 83, giving her one delegate. The Obama group totals 150, giving him two delegates. Biden, Richardson, and Dodd aren't viable, which leaves one delegate up for grabs.

After determining viability, supporters have thirty minutes to "realign." This is when caucusing gets interesting and intense. Our mission is to get Edwards that remaining delegate, so we need to bring more supporters into our room.

Determining how many more supporters we need involves an equation: Number of Supporters times Number of Delegates at Stake divided by Number of Caucus Participants equals Number of Delegates for a Candidate, rounded up. Ninety-two supporters give us 1.19, which equals one delegate. We need 116 to get to 1.5, which, rounded up, will give us the extra delegate. Carter double-checks the math. We're 24 folks short.

With Richardson's supporters gathered in a room next to ours and Biden's in the church foyer, we instantly dispatch people to persuade them to realign with Edwards. One on one, we pitch Edwards's vision, passion, programs, integrity, and electability. (These qualities will not be in question until Edwards's illicit affair comes to light and he admits to it in August 2008.) We pick up 15 of Richardson's people to reach 107, but we still needed 9 more. The clock is ticking.

The precinct captain for Biden wants us to give him some Edwards supporters so Biden can become "viable" and at least get one delegate.

Interesting strategy. Not going to happen. After a spirited exchange with him, I return to the Edwards group and ask, "Who's willing to work on this guy?"

A lady in our group stands up and says, "I will! I'm his wife," and she strolls from the room to gales of laughter and hearty applause.

At that point, another supporter in our group, clutching an iPhone, says, "Look at this! Early returns show Edwards leading Obama and Hillary."

I say, "Come with me."

The triplets are shadowing us, mesmerized. They understand what's going on. The campaigns are teams. This is a competition. There are goals. For them, it's like a sporting event. The process is visceral and immediate; our goal is clear.

We wade into the Biden group again and announce that we have news. With pressure coming from several directions, Biden's supporters are softening. They like Edwards and, after weighing the merits, the fact that time is running out and at least one marriage is on the line, they start to move.

One by one, Biden's supporters walk into our room—16 in all—to thunderous applause and cheers, bringing the Edwards total to 123 (1.5932 on the calculator), winning Edwards that second delegate.

As the final counts are recorded, we feel moved to be part of this group of Americans standing up for their presidential candidates in this vibrant demonstration of democracy in action. As we walk out to our car, arms filled with posters, buttons, tape, and leftover snacks, the boys say they can't believe what they've just seen us do. "You guys were amazing," Jackson says.

Back at our hotel in Des Moines, the results are coming in. The winner of the 2008 Iowa Caucuses is Barack Obama; Edwards comes in second; Hillary comes in third.

*Spring 2008*

The triplets are thirteen and finishing seventh grade. They're trying out for the junior lifeguard program run by the Los Angeles County Fire Department. The program instructs youth in beach and ocean skills such as water safety, physical conditioning, first aid, rescue techniques, CPR, and more. It's a rigorous program that requires all applicants to pass a timed swimming test in an Olympic-size pool before being put through exercises and trials on the beach and in the open ocean.

To qualify, the guys need to swim one hundred yards in under one minute and forty seconds. We get them some private instruction in advance to get them ready. On the day of the time trials, they dive in with gusto. Jackson comes in at one minute thirty-five seconds; Braden's best time is one minute thirty-six seconds; Carter's first and best time is one minute twenty-six seconds. They're in.

The program runs all summer and involves the junior guards meeting at the beach each day to work out and do drills. They don't serve as lifeguards, but their training, if they stick with it, could lead to one day becoming lifeguards.

All three of our boys are strong swimmers. They've had a fair amount of experience bodysurfing and boogie board surfing in the ocean. But junior guard training is educational, not recreational. For example, during one of their drills, the kids must swim out to a buoy that's more than a hundred yards offshore. The water is choppy. Jackson takes in a mouthful of ocean and gags but has to keep swimming. When they reach the buoy, the kids must swim back. Jackson has broad shoulders and a strong upper body, so he's able to power through, but the drill is scary. Carter, strong and fast, toughs it out. Braden perseveres. But the guys come home exhausted and clear that junior guards is no "day at the beach"—it's a test of fortitude and endurance.

*September 2008*

The sky is falling.

Three months before what will be our third year on 3rd Street in Manhattan Beach, the federal government is taking over two financial institutions, Fannie Mae and Freddie Mac, which own or guarantee almost half of the $12 trillion home mortgage market in the US. Practically every home mortgage lender and every Wall Street bank you can name has relied on these two institutions to underwrite the entire home financing industry in America. On top of that, investors worldwide own over $5 trillion—nearly half—of the debt that Fannie and Freddie guarantee.

The result is panic. We're aware because we have two loans on our house: a first from Countrywide, and a home equity line of credit (HELOC) with Bank of America that funded most of the renovation. (Countrywide and its CEO, Angelo Mozilo, will ultimately be accused of "luring borrowers into taking mortgages they didn't understand." Before Countrywide can fail completely, it will be acquired by Bank of America.)

My mother and father are long gone, but they would recognize the sense of dread that's sweeping the country. Like so many millions of Americans of their generation, they were permanently scarred by the Great Depression. My mother was convinced there was going to be another stock market crash during her lifetime. She was so certain of it that she was opposed to investing in anything except the houses we lived in. "Mark my words," she'd say. "There's going to be another crash." She was so adamant that I couldn't resist teasing her. I said, "Mom, if you die before there's another stock market crash, we're going to put on your tombstone, 'Here lies Virginia Boon Casady, who crashed before the market did.'" She laughed. A great, big laugh.

Mom died on July 5, 1987. The US stock market crashed less than four months later on October 22. In the five years running up to the 1987 crash, known as "Black Monday," the Dow Jones Industrial Average

(DJIA) had more than tripled. Some believe the crash was caused by *irrational* behavior on the part of investors. Other analysts believe that excessive stock prices and computerized trading were the cause. Whatever the cause, we gave Mom the benefit of the doubt—the market crashed about the same time she did.

When something as big as the US economy collapses, it sends shock waves everywhere. Even in our house. Barbara has a wealthy client for whom she's designing a second home in Sandpoint, Idaho. His stock portfolio has taken a major hit; he tells her, "Don't buy another thing." I'm working on a musical tribute to R&B legend Smokey Robinson benefiting the United Negro College Fund (UNCF), and the sponsors are pulling out.

One week later, Wall Street comes apart at the seams. Lehman Brothers, one of the biggest banks on "The Street," collapses, and the dominoes keep tumbling—AIG, Merrill Lynch, Wachovia, Bear Stearns, Countrywide. At thirteen-turning-fourteen, the triplets are old enough to know something terrible is happening. They can see it in our eyes and hear it in our voices as we wake up to the truth that we are all living at the mercy of behemoth banks, giant insurance companies, and a few hundred "titans of Wall Street," and they're all spinning out of control.

In 2008, companies described as "too big to fail" are failing and, oddly, everyone seems surprised. Even Alan Greenspan, the chairman of the Federal Reserve from 1987 to 2006, regarded as an "economic sage" and nicknamed the "Maestro" for his economic acumen, is surprised. Three years after stepping down as chairman of the Federal Reserve, the humbled, eighty-three-year-old Greenspan admits to a congressional committee that he "put too much faith in the self-correcting power of free markets and had failed to anticipate the self-destructive power of wanton mortgage lending." In effect, he's saying, and I'm paraphrasing here, he never thought American companies would ever do anything that wasn't in their best interests. Did this man ever hear of the Great Depression? (Surely, he did.) Wasn't he around for the savings and loan debacle in the 1980s? (He was.) Does he remember "Black Monday?" (He must.) Didn't he witness the dot-com crash in 2000? (He did.)

## *October 2008*

A month later, and roughly three months before the triplets' fourteenth birthday, we are quaking in our financial boots over something we had nothing to do with. America is diving into the deepest global economic crisis since the Great Depression of 1929. Working people by the millions are losing their jobs, their homes, and their businesses.

President George W. Bush signs the Emergency Economic Stabilization Act, creating the now-infamous $700 billion dollar "Troubled Assets Relief Program," nicknamed "TARP." I always thought the name was ironic. When I was growing up, a tarp was something you threw over the woodpile or an old car when you wanted to hide it. This TARP was created to purchase the "toxic," as in worthless, assets of US banks that were deemed "too big to fail"—banks like Bank of America, JPMorgan Chase, Wells Fargo, and Citigroup—so they won't disintegrate.

These are dark times that we wish we could shield our children from, but they are also times we hope they will learn from when they become adults.

## *Grinding*

The boys announce that there's a school dance at the community center near us and they want to go. They're in eighth grade at Manhattan Beach Middle School—fourteen years old. They've been to a cotillion, but they haven't been to a school dance before, so we're taking them. As we arrive, we notice several parents dropping off their *daughters* and driving away. We've got boys, but we're parking and going in with them to have a look.

What we see is mind-boggling. Music of the day is pounding, and the dance floor is filled with young boys grinding up against the backsides of young girls. Very suggestive—make that sexual—and none of the adults who are present seem to mind. If we had a daughter, there's no way she would be at this dance. We've got boys, and we don't want them at this dance. We're aghast—and disapproving. We tell the boys we don't want them grinding, that it's inappropriate and disrespectful to the girls; then we retreat to the sidelines to watch. The boys have fun dancing, without grinding, and we file the whole affair under "Things We Never Thought We'd See." (Years later, we learn that grinding is so pervasive and provocative that many schools stop having dances or they require parents and students to sign contracts, in advance, stipulating the type of music and dancing allowed.)

*Fall 2009*

The triplets are high school freshmen, meeting their freshman baseball coach, Brad Angeleri, for the first time. Coach Angeleri announces practices will be five days a week, from 3:00 p.m. to 5:30 or 6:00 p.m. After the formal part of the meeting, we introduce ourselves. Barb asks whether Tuesday practices can be finished a few minutes before 6:00 p.m. When the coach asks why, Barb explains that the boys have piano lessons on Tuesdays at 6:00. I look at the boys; they look at me. I'm thinking, *Oh jeez. Mom's asking the coach for an exception for our kids, which we never do, and the reason she's giving is piano lessons!* The boys and I are staring at the ground.

"Piano lessons, huh?" the coach says. "Wouldn't want baseball practice to interfere with their piano lessons." A beat. Then, looking at the boys: "No problem."

Asking for the guys to get out of baseball practice early for piano lessons *may* not be our best look, but Barb is pleased, and the boys seem fine with it. They know their mother.

*Spring 2009*

The triplets are playing together on the freshman team. Typically, Jackson in the outfield, Braden in the infield, Carter pitching. Major League Baseball is rife with pitchers who are solid batters, in some cases spectacular batters, but for some reason, the coaches are not allowing Carter to hit. Finally, near the end of the season, in a game against one of the worst teams in the league, Carter is allowed one at-bat. He hits a homerun on the varsity field, the school's largest.

Meanwhile, Coach Angeleri lets it be known that his birthday's coming up. That summer, the boys decide to give him a special present. With the help of their piano teacher, Megan, they learn how to play "Take Me Out to the Ballgame" together on the piano, sitting side by side, each playing a different piano part but singing in unison. We make a video. They're wearing their baseball uniforms, playing and singing the song and, at the end, they look at the camera and say, "Happy Birthday, Coach." We transfer their performance to a DVD.

Later, the guys are playing in a baseball tournament, facing a team led by Coach Angeleri. The triplets' team defeats the coach's team decisively with the Casady Brothers contributing to the win with their gloves and bats. After the game, I walk over to Angeleri. Feeling the sting of defeat, he says, "Does your family have a dog?"

"No. Why?"

"'Cause if you had a dog, it would probably bite me right now!"

I hand him the DVD and say, "Here you go. The boys made this for your birthday."

Weeks later, Coach Angeleri tells us he was genuinely touched by the triplets' gift. He says he's never received anything like it before.

### April 15, 2009

Attorney General Eric Holder is addressing the grand opening conference of West Point's Center for the Rule of Law. This is notable because Attorney General Holder is the first African American to serve as attorney general of the United States and because he was appointed by Barack Obama, the first African American president of the United States, elected in November 2008.

At fourteen, our boys are aware that the election of Barack Obama marks an historic moment in America. And they like Obama. They think he's cool. At the moment, though, they're probably not aware of the importance of Attorney General Holder's speech about one of the formational pillars of our democracy.

In his remarks, Mr. Holder says, "As Americans, we *all* bear a special responsibility to both uphold and promote the rule of law. This sacred responsibility springs from our unique place in history, and it is the animating force of our heritage—and of our destiny—as a nation." He's exactly right. Reason and justice form the foundation of our freedoms; together, they inform the idea that America is a nation of *laws*, not men.

The concept that *no person is above the law* simply does not exist in many countries. Visit Mexico, for example, get pulled over by a policeman and, under certain circumstances, a generous bribe—*el soborno* or *la mordida* in Spanish—will enable you to skirt the law. Try the same thing in the United States and 99 percent of the time, you'll go directly to jail for it. Why? Because we are a nation of *laws* and, for the most part, no one, no matter how rich, powerful, or well-positioned, is above the law. True, there have been exceptions. Great, ghastly exceptions. Sometimes, even those sworn to uphold the law break it. But throughout our tumultuous and messy history, the overarching concept that no one is above the law has been fought for, defended, and largely maintained.

There are two other essential pillars that created the America my father grew up in and the America he left to me and my brothers: freedom of the press and the separation of church and state. Growing up in a newspaper family, I have a profound regard for freedom of the press. Even as television news has grown to prominence, it has followed the traditions of journalism established by newspapers. Indeed, legacy newspapers like the *New York Times* and the *Washington Post* still break stories on a daily basis that provide the fuel for network TV news broadcasts and commentary.

Without open, uncensored reporting, without newspapers, magazines, internet blogs, and television news that adheres to the principles of journalism and is free from government intervention and manipulation, our democratic institutions cannot be maintained. A free press exists to shine a light on business, the economy, government, our culture, our laws and practices, strengths and failings. The brilliance of that light protects us all. The masthead of the *Washington Post* says it best: "Democracy Dies in Darkness."

As for the separation of church and state, one need only look to the brutal and incessant unrest in the Middle East to find an urgent argument for this pillar. In most Middle Eastern countries, religious beliefs are inseparable from political and policy positions. The needs and wants of the nation-states are collapsed inside and on top of its religious beliefs and practices, each religious group fighting for dominance and, when they achieve it, working to suppress the others. Where there is no separation of church and state in governance, the result is chaos, unrest, war, even genocide. And there will be no end to it so long as the guiding principle of the separation of church and state is not understood, officially adopted, and completely adhered to.

Note to our children's generation and those that will follow: These pillars—the rule of law, a free press, and the separation of church and state—all of which seemed strong and unassailable in the America I grew up in, are now in danger. In today's America, we must work to guard them and keep them from being undermined. These are indispensable guardrails that protect our experiment in democracy, and they're worth fighting for.

*June 2009*

As summer approaches, Barbara is asking the boys whether they want to enroll in junior guards again. They did it last summer and got a lot out of it. Given that we live near the ocean and they're budding surfers, it's a smart thing to do.

But we're not getting any buy-in. Seeming to speak for his brothers, Jackson says, "I don't want to do junior guards again."

Barbara ups the ante. "All right, then, how about Boy Scouts?"

Without missing a beat, Jackson shoots back, "So now you're threatening me with a uniform and camping?"

It's clear the boys have minds of their own. They want to do what *they* want to do. And they're not doing junior guards again. Or the Boy Scouts.

*Chapter 9*

# THE ROAD AHEAD

> *Change will not come if we wait for some other person
> or some other time. We are the ones we've been waiting for.
> We are the change that we seek.*
> —PRESIDENT BARACK OBAMA

When the wheels came off the US economy and the global economy in 2008, the triplets were barely teenagers. Ever since, we've been talking to them about the need for guardrails in life. Guardrails work. But a lot of the guardrails in America have been taken down.

In a country without guardrails, devastating things can happen.

*January 20, 2010*

For example, a giant guardrail is coming down in 2010, two weeks after the boys turn fifteen. In Citizens United vs. Federal Election Commission, the US Supreme Court rules that the free speech clause of the First Amendment prohibits the government from restricting independent expenditures for political campaigns by corporations, including nonprofit corporations, labor unions, and political action committees (PACs). The decision effectively unleashes a tsunami of billions of dollars in so-called dark money from largely secretive donors who, ten years later, continue to dominate political campaigns. In other words, the court not only invalidates all previous attempts to get big money out of politics but instead guarantees that big money will control politics and politicians in America for the foreseeable future.

Why do we need to get big money, dark money, out of politics? Why do we need guardrails and intelligent regulation? Because our free enterprise system has a history of getting out of control. In the 1900s. In the 1920s. In the 1930s. The 1980s. In 2000. In 2008. History shows that every so often, we learn we can't trust ourselves to police ourselves, so we look, as we should, to our government to protect us from ourselves. And the truth is that informed, intelligent, consistently enforced regulations have worked very well for a very long time. Indeed, up until about forty years ago, utilities were regulated, Wall Street was regulated, banks were regulated, insurance companies were regulated, airlines were regulated, even television was regulated. And until 2010, there were laws limiting contributions to political campaigns. Big money couldn't buy and sell America's politicians like it can now. History proves that sensible regulations save lives, save companies, and save fortunes. And getting dark money out of politics might save democracy.

### *April 5, 2010*

But wait, there's more. On April 5, 2010, as baseball season is getting underway in Manhattan Beach, in Montcoal, West Virginia, a huge underground explosion blamed on methane gas has killed twenty-nine coal miners in the deadliest US mining disaster in nearly four decades. The sprawling Upper Big Branch Mine, a part of Massey Energy Company, had a significant history of safety violations, including fifty-seven infractions for, among other things, not properly ventilating highly combustible methane gas.

At the end of the year, the CEO of Massey Energy will announce his retirement with a package worth $12 million. Before he leaves, he offers the families of the twenty-nine miners who died $3 million per family—a total of $87 million. Three million for each dead miner and twelve million for one executive who faked the safety records that led to their deaths.

Two weeks after the mine explosion in West Virginia, on the evening of April 20, 2010, an explosion and fire engulf the Deepwater Horizon, a drilling platform operated by British Petroleum (BP) some fifty miles off the coast of Louisiana, killing eleven workers and causing the worst oil spill in US history. When the well's so-called "blowout preventer," located more than two miles below the ocean's surface, fails, over 170 million gallons of toxic crude will pour into the Gulf of Mexico for three months, devastating fish, wildlife habitat, the local economy, and altering the basic health and welfare of the entire region.

The National Commission on the BP Deepwater Horizon Oil Spill and Offshore Drilling, established by President Obama to investigate the disaster, concludes that the oil well blowout was preventable and that the cause of the disaster "could be traced to a series of identifiable mistakes made by the companies operating the well—BP, Halliburton, and Transocean—that reveal such systematic failures in risk management that they place in doubt the safety culture of the entire industry." A subsequent analysis by Det Norske Veritas (DNV) concludes that the blowout preventer on the BP well, a device that is standard on all such deepwater wells, was not designed to prevent such a disaster.

What do the West Virginia coal mine disaster and the Deepwater Horizon disaster have in common? Try profit over safety. Try greed.

*Summer 2010*

As high school freshmen, the boys played together on the frosh-soph baseball team, and the team won a lot of games. The roster was strong from end to end. Now, in July and August following their freshman year, the triplets are on a Senior Little League team (ages thirteen to sixteen) that's hoping to play its way to the 2010 Senior Little League World Series in Bangor, Maine. The "beach team" is powerful, delivering strong hitting, fielding, and pitching. Not only is Carter among the pitchers but, in a key game in Ontario that the Manhattan Beach guys must win to advance, he throws a two-hit shutout paving the road to Bangor, marking the first time a Manhattan Beach team has ever made it to the playoffs. In Maine, after winning fifteen games in a row to get there and defeating Aruba, the team that goes on to win the series, the MB team loses to the Bangor team, which has been resting while the boys from the beach have been playing and traveling nonstop. All in all, it's an impressive run and an unforgettable summer of baseball. All the Manhattan Beach players come home with great memories and strong stats.

*September 2010*

The Casady Brothers are sophomores in high school, and they're being invited to try out for the high school surf team. "Surf P.E." involves getting up at 5:30 a.m., meeting at the beach at 6:30 a.m., three times a week, and swimming in cold water, sometimes in the dark. The surfers call it "dawn patrol." Braden and Jackson want to do it. Carter doesn't like cold water or getting up at five-thirty in the morning. He and I like body surfing in warm water on sunny days. Barbara and I take Carter's separation from his brothers as an example of the boys beginning to individuate and distinguish themselves from each other.

Jackson and Braden don't surf on longboards, but they've gotten good at riding bodyboards (aka "boogie boards"). They're so good, in fact, that the coach asks them to join the surf team. To everyone's surprise, over the coming months and years, the Casady Brothers become the surf team's secret weapon, since the other teams in the South Bay don't have designated body boarders. In a pitched competition, after Mira Costa's board surfers have racked up as many points as possible, the coach puts Jackson and Braden in the water to rack up a few more. Invariably, the other teams put longboard surfers in to compete with our boys on the shorter, wider bodyboards, and Jackson and Braden take first and second place almost every time, immediately bumping up our team's score.

After one meet, the surf coach asks me, "Are your boys' backs hurting them?"

I say, "No, I don't think so. Why do you ask?"

He says, "They should, because they're carrying the team!"

One day after school, on September 9, 2010, at around 6:00 p.m. Pacific time, a massive leak in a natural gas pipeline operated by the Pacific Gas and Electric Company (PG&E), explodes in a neighborhood in San Bruno, California, near San Francisco, killing eight people and destroying thirty-eight homes.

Sound familiar?

An investigation into the San Bruno tragedy by the National Transportation Safety Board (NTSB), which also responds to pipeline disasters, found "baffling mistakes" and a lack of monitoring by regulators who placed "blind trust" in the utility to conduct its business safely. The report concluded that poor pipeline welds went undetected because of a lack of inspections by the company and inadequate monitoring by what few state and federal regulators still existed. PG&E also lacked a workable emergency response plan that could have helped prevent the devastation, including failure by the utility to shut off the leaking gas for ninety-five minutes after the explosion.

Can you see a pattern here?

The NTSB concludes that, while the cause may have been "technical" and was an "organizational accident," the state utility commission had exempted all natural gas pipelines built before 1961 from pressure testing, and the federal government did the same for pipelines built before 1970. That's right—forty and fifty-year-old high-pressure gas pipelines, critical pieces of our infrastructure, exempt from testing.

*December 10, 2010*

Senator Bernie Sanders (I-Vermont) is on the floor of the US Senate giving a speech that will last over eight and half hours and become a book (*The Speech*). Here's what he's saying: after the 2008 meltdown, while millions of Americans were losing their assets and we were quaking in our distressed financial boots, the largest corporations on the planet were receiving massive bailouts.

On October 6, 2008, the Federal Reserve Bank ("the Fed") announced it would loan *$900 billion* to those failing banks. Sanders, a three-time candidate for president, discovers it was much, much more. In *The Speech*, Senator Sanders recounts that Wall Street giant Goldman Sachs alone received nearly $780 billion from the Fed. Morgan Stanley received over $2 trillion. Citigroup got $2.4 trillion. Bear Stearns received nearly $1 trillion. Merrill Lynch received $2.2 trillion in short term loans from the Fed.

One day later, on October 7, the Fed moved to lend $1.3 trillion to several companies and entities *outside* the US financial sector. The Federal Reserve Bank bailed out the Korea Development Bank by purchasing $2 billion of its commercial paper. While businesses large and small were cratering in the US, our "national bank" was helping Korea? The Arab

Banking Corporation received over $23 billion in loans with interest as low as one quarter of 1 percent. The Fed extended over $9.6 billion to the Banco de México. ¡Ay caramba!

A report issued by the United States Senate—*The Levin-Coburn Report*—concludes that "the [2008 financial] crisis was not a natural disaster, but the result of high risk, complex financial products; undisclosed conflicts of interest; and the failure of regulators, the credit rating agencies, and the market itself to rein in the excesses of Wall Street."

*The excesses of Wall Street.* Wait. That sounds disturbingly familiar. Is it possible those excesses were motivated by greed?

Pardon me if I mount my soap box again, but part of what I want this book to do is open eyes and point to what's really going on. It's time to reform American capitalism top to bottom. I talk to our teenage sons about it, and I don't intend to stop. Expecting companies to make ever-increasing profits for stockholders, every quarter, in a system that's designed to favor billionaires at the expense of average workers, is not working. And it hasn't worked, except for billionaires, for decades. It's time for transformational change. There's nothing wrong with capitalism that top-to-bottom reform and judicious regulations can't fix.

When we decided to accept responsibility for having triplets and everything that might entail, we also accepted responsibility for the world we're bringing them into and, at some point, telling them the truth about that world. As a father, I couldn't write this book without commenting, along the way, on what's happening in the country that surrounds them and us. We wish we were leaving our sons a kinder, gentler, more just and sustainable world. But we're not. Make no mistake: the America we've leaving to our children and their children is a remarkable country brimming with unrealized potential; it's also flawed, in turmoil, in danger, and at a critical moment in its history. As America faces hard truths about its past and an uncertain future, our sons' generation, and the generations following them, will face a world full of ups and down, triumphs and sorrows.

*February 12, 2011*

One of my oldest friends, Shannon Green, died today. We met in high school. I was looking for someone to play upright bass in my folk music group. The head of the high school music department recommended Shannon. So I knocked on his door one Saturday morning. Shannon answered in his bathrobe, bed hair going in various directions, holding a cup of coffee and smoking a cigarette. I thought, "Wow, he must be a *real* musician." He was.

*March 2011*

Across forty-eight years, I don't think there was ever a time when I was with Shannon when we didn't sing and play music. That was our bond. That and liberal politics. Now, Shannon's wife of thirty-five years, Merry Ann, also a treasured friend, is calling to ask whether we can come up to San Francisco and help her empty out Shan's office. We say "sure."

The triplets are sophomores in high school. And for the first time, we're going to be leaving them alone for two nights. We trust them. But they're sixteen. And they're boys. So I tell them they can't have any girls over while we're gone. I also mention to our next-door neighbor, Nancy, that we're going to be away for a couple of nights. Her kitchen window is about twelve feet below our kitchen window. (Upside-down house.) I tell her why we're going and ask her to "keep an ear out." Especially for high-pitched female voices. She understands.

We fly to San Francisco and connect with Merry Ann. That evening, having cleared out Shannon's office, we're having a glass of wine when my phone rings. It's Heidi, our neighbor across the street from Nancy.

Nancy doesn't have our cell number, so she called Heidi to report hearing animated voices in our kitchen. "Sounds like a party."

Our boys know Heidi and her husband, Jay, very well, and I often loan them tapes and DVDs. So we suggest that Heidi go to our house and ask if she can pick up a DVD in my office that I've offered to loan them. The front door is unlocked; Heidi makes a beeline for the kitchen. When she walks in, she's confused. The large center island that is usually covered with plants and kitchen items is now covered with dozens of red plastic cups. Braden and Jackson are there, along with several of their teenage boy and girl friends. Heidi quickly takes in the scene, tells the guys, "This isn't cool," exits, and calls us back.

It looks like a party, all right, she reports, describing the scene. We don't know what's going on except that our sons have invited their friends over while we're out of town, against our clear instructions not to do so. With Barbara and Merry Ann looking on, I call Jackson on his cell phone. He says, oh yes, they're having a few friends over and casually mentions they're playing beer pong, and it will be breaking up pretty soon. The way Jackson describes the gathering is nonchalant and reassuring—and yes, there are some girls. I tell him to inform everyone that the party's over and send everybody home. He says he will. I hang up, turn to Barb and Merry Ann and ask, "What's beer pong?"

After a quick Google search, we discover, of course, that beer pong is a drinking game played with red plastic cups and a ping-pong ball. Now, our shock turns to dread. There's been a party at our house with underage kids playing a drinking game; we're not there, and we're liable should anything happen. Barbara says, "I'm going home. Right now." Then she asks Merry Ann, "Can you get me on a flight?"

Merry Ann has been a management level employee with American Airlines for decades. She taps her phone a few times and announces that

Barb is on the next flight to Los Angeles. Barbara grabs her purse, and Merry Ann gives her a ride to the airport.

Meanwhile, on 3rd Street, the party has broken up. Braden and Jackson, the hosts, have cleaned up. Mostly. (I will find a million red plastic cups in the recycling can the next day.) Carter, we'll find out later, took a dim view of the idea from the outset and sequestered himself in the kids' TV room the whole time. When the last teenager has gone, Jackson and Braden join him.

Barely three hours after Nancy called Heidi and Heidi called us, Barbara walks through the front door of our house, goes straight to the TV room, and steps in. Barb says the look on the boys' faces was one of stunned disbelief.

"We thought you were in San Francisco."

"I was."

Barbara lectures the boys about the dangers associated with their "party," she expresses our disappointment that they've betrayed our trust while we were helping Merry Ann in her time of grief, and she sends the guys to bed with a promise: "We will discuss this further, in detail, in the morning, and there will be consequences. Now give me your phones."

I've often told the triplets, "Don't mess with your mother." They are quite clear this evening that they have.

Barbara retires to our bedroom with a yellow notepad and a pen; she opens each of the boys' cellphones and writes down the names of everyone they called and/or texted before, during, and after the party, compiling a list of the attendees. At some point, she discovers the party even had a name: "The Big Shebang."

The next morning, there's a full airing of the whole alarming affair. Barb takes the boys through their guest list, name by name. They're pleading: "Please don't call the parents." To which Barbara replies, in effect, when you break the rules, when you betray our trust, you don't get to say how this goes.

Barbara knows the parents of most of the kids well enough to call them. In one case, she knows enough *not* to call. The mom of one of the boys' friends is going through a divorce; Barbara knows if she blows the whistle on the son and his dad finds out, it could have serious ramifications in a brewing custody battle.

The triplets are grounded. Cell phones will not be returned for three weeks. Each boy is required to write an essay explaining what he did and why it was dangerous. Even though his brothers make it clear Carter did not participate, Barbara makes it clear he also did nothing to stop them or alert us. He needs to write about that.

By the time I return from San Francisco the next day, the triplets have been busted, thoroughly reprimanded, educated, and disciplined by their mother. You go, Barb!

Shannon would have loved this story; he would've especially enjoyed being the cause of it, but he probably would have given the boys hell for interrupting our visit. It makes me miss him more.

*Virginia*

I wish our kids had met their Grandma Casady. Like Barbara, she was a force to be reckoned with. My mother became a realtor in 1963, at the age of fifty-five. She did it to support the California Fair Housing Act (the Rumford Act), which was passed by the California legislature that year to end racial discrimination by property owners and landlords. My mom's new job was my introduction to the fact that there was something called systemic racism in America. I was sixteen.

Mom would come home and tell us about taking her Black clients to see houses that were listed for sale in white neighborhoods. Once they were inside, she would introduce herself and her clients. The minute the listing agent realized that the potential buyers were African American, the agent would say, "Oh, I'm very sorry, Mrs. Casady, but this house has already sold."

One time, Mother left her clients in the car and went into the house alone.

"Hi, I'm Virginia Casady with Fletcher Hills Realty. Is this house still for sale?"

"Oh, yes!" came the answer.

"Wonderful," Mother said. "I'll be right back. I need to get something from the car."

She returned, of course, with her African American clients, to the astonishment of the listing agent who had no choice but to show the house and sell it to her clients, if they wanted it. Because it was the law.

Mom led by example. She didn't just sell houses to Black families in other white neighborhoods; she sold a house to a Black family on our street. Some of our neighbors were upset, but everybody got over it soon enough. When I asked her one day why people were prejudiced, Mom went to the record player, put on the vinyl Broadway cast recording from the musical *South Pacific*, and had us listen to "You've Got to Be Carefully Taught" written by Richard Rodgers and Oscar Hammerstein.

> *You've got to be carefully taught*
> *You've got to be taught to hate and fear*
> *You've got to be taught from year to year*
> *It's got to be drummed in your dear little ear*
> *You've got to be carefully taught*
> *You've got to be taught to be afraid*
> *Of people whose eyes are oddly made*
> *And people whose skin is a different shade*
> *You've got to be carefully taught*
>
> © Williamson Music. All rights reserved. Used with permission.

Mom made sure we were being taught not to hate and fear or be suspicious of people whose skin was a different shade. She was making sure that job got done. When I asked her why there was so much racism in the South where the civil rights movement was growing, she said, "Unfortunately, that's how many people in the South are taught." Obviously, that's how some of the homeowners and realtors who were resisting the Fair Housing Act in California had been taught as well.

In 2011, forty-eight years after my mother became a realtor to work on behalf of open housing, she would be horrified by the pervasive racial injustice that still exists in America. That is embedded in America. She would be the first to point out that however much progress toward racial justice we've made since she became a realtor—and we've made some—it has not been complete enough, systemic enough, or permanent enough. My generation, our sons' generation, and generations to come must stand up and act to end systemic racism for good. The time for justice is now.

*Driving*

At sixteen, Braden, Carter, and Jackson are old enough to get driver's licenses, after they satisfy several state requirements. First, they have to take a California driver's education course. Check. They are allowed to have provisional learner's permits for at least six months. Check. They need to fulfill six hours of driver's training behind the wheel with an instructor. Check. And they're each supposed to log fifty hours of practice driving, ten of them at night, with an adult who is at least twenty-five years old. Haven't done that. Finally, they'll need to pass a written test and a road test at the Department of Motor Vehicles (DMV).

The boys hear that a lot of their friends' parents aren't requiring the fifty hours of practice driving. Running errands around Manhattan Beach doesn't exactly rack up a lot of driving time, especially in our case, when it's divided by three. This could take years.

We decide to go for the practice hours, so we're taking a road trip: Manhattan Beach to Lake Havasu City, Arizona, 330 miles; Lake Havasu to the Grand Canyon, another almost 330 miles; then from the Grand Canyon to Hoover Dam, about 100 miles; Hoover Dam to Las Vegas, 40 miles; and Las Vegas back to Manhattan Beach, nearly 300 miles.

We figure that after driving roughly eleven hundred miles, the boys will have logged enough practice time behind the wheel at various times, on various types of roads. And while one of them drives, one of us will sit in the passenger seat wearing a crash helmet and a flame-retardant NASCAR suit.

The drive to Lake Havasu is long. As they take turns behind the wheel, the guys seem nervous at first, especially when navigating freeway transitions, but they relax as the hours pass. Lake Havasu is beautiful, and the hotel offers adult guests a cocktail when registering. While doing a bit of sightseeing, the guys are surprised to learn that the London Bridge has been moved here from England, linking the mainland to marinas and a path known as "the Island." We sleep well; the fellas are exhausted from driving.

The next day, the boys drive us to the Grand Canyon. We know it will be late when we arrive, so we arrange to stay at a modest motel a few miles from the canyon. In the morning, on our way to the rim, we stop at the famous Cameron Trading Post, which was established in 1916. The boys are intrigued by the trading post's gallery and gift shop offering unique Native American art and locally made items. The canyon itself is breathtaking, of course, and the Grand Canyon Museum Collection is fascinating.

The next day, as we tour Hoover Dam, it's hard not be moved by its magnificence. Dwarfed by its size and impressed with the technological achievements and human sacrifices that made its construction possible, the boys are wide-eyed at this extraordinary example of what Americans can do when we work together as a nation.

I take the opportunity to talk to them about how we can do better, about how great America *used* to be when we shared big goals and worked together to achieve them. I point out that, in the post-Depression America my brothers and I grew up in, our government built a national highway system that literally paved the way for the trucking and automobile industries to prosper in this country. We built airports that enabled the airline industry to take off and grow. The collective "we" built the public schools where my brothers and I were educated and the boys are going to school. We put a man on the moon.

University of British Columbia anthropologist Wade Davis makes the point better than I ever could in a *Rolling Stone* magazine article titled "The Unraveling of America." Davis uses World War II as an example: "In 1940, with Europe already ablaze, the United States had a smaller army than either Portugal or Bulgaria," Davis writes. "Within four years, 18 million men and women would serve in uniform, with millions more working double shifts in mines and factories that made America, as President Roosevelt promised, the arsenal of democracy."

In recent times, Americans have largely forgotten what it is to sacrifice for our country; some even claim it's too much to get vaccinated or wear a face mask to prevent the spread of a global pandemic. And yet, Davis notes, "When the Japanese, within six weeks of Pearl Harbor, took control of 90 percent of the world's rubber supply, the US dropped the speed limit to 35 mph to protect tires, and then, in three years, invented from scratch a synthetic-rubber industry that allowed Allied armies to roll over the Nazis. At its peak, Henry Ford's Willow Run Plant produced a B-24 Liberator every two hours, around the clock. Shipyards in Long Beach and Sausalito spat out Liberty ships at a rate of two a day for four years; the record was a ship built in four days, 15 hours and 29 minutes.

A single American factory, Chrysler's Detroit Arsenal, built more tanks than the whole of the Third Reich." Americans willingly made sacrifices and stepped up to meet a global threat.

I gave up on the idea of working in government long ago, but our sons know I'm a political activist, so we talk about politics and policy. In 2011, as we take our driving trip, we're talking about the fact that the US is still digging out of a deep economic ditch. Nationally, unemployment is 9 percent and, depending on the figures you use, between thirteen and fifteen million Americans are still out of work or underemployed. Experts estimate that the US urgently needs to invest at least $3 trillion in infrastructure—roads, bridges, schools, water and sewer systems, rural broadband internet, a smart electric grid, etc. Will we invest in America and American workers to meet this challenge? As Wade Davis notes, "Since 2001, the US has spent over $6 trillion on military operations and war, money that might have been invested in infrastructure at home. China, meanwhile, built its nation, pouring more cement every three years than America did in the entire 20th century."

So let's put a pin in this: America has big needs; let's have big goals.

At the last stop on our driving trip, Las Vegas, we see Blue Man Group perform; the guys love their outsized antics. We observe the obvious excesses of Vegas from a safe distance and spend the night in an enormous, opulent suite to which we were upgraded. The next morning, we're treated to a spectacular panoramic view of the desert, aglow in the light of a new day, before the boys drive us back to Manhattan Beach.

Maybe it's Vegas and all that it conjures, or maybe it's because our boys are becoming young men, but we're realizing that among the many experiences they will have without us, and already have had, are their interactions and relationships with women. By the time Braden, Carter, and Jackson finish college, the world will be reverberating with revelations of sexual misconduct by all sorts of famous and powerful men busted during the #MeToo Movement, which had its beginnings back in 2006, as our sons were entering middle school.

On a personal note, and it's an important one, because we have boys, Barbara and I have long had our attention on raising young men who would be mindful and respectful of women. We have strived to make sure our sons understand that women deserve to be heard and that no means no. Power does not entitle men or women to have their way with those who are less powerful or intimidated by power. So, gentlemen, if you become powerful and influential men during your lifetimes, and you might, your mother and I request that, as good, intelligent, caring men, you live by the principle that women *and* men deserve to be respected and heard. Your power, position, or influence, should you have any, does not give you any special rights over others. As a society, we need to restore dignity and respect to the way we think about, talk about, and treat each other.

## Chapter 10

# THIS CHANGES EVERYTHING

> *We cannot always build the future for our youth, but we can build our youth for the future.*
> —US PRESIDENT FRANKLIN D. ROOSEVELT

I'm borrowing the title of this chapter, "This Changes Everything," from Naomi Klein's landmark book about the climate emergency that threatens our survival on planet Earth.

So this is the laugh-out-loud, feel-good chapter.

*February 26, 2012*

I'm thinking about my mother and how she introduced me to the fact that there's systemic racism in America when I was sixteen. I'm thinking about her because there's a story on every TV newscast tonight about a gun-toting vigilante named George Zimmerman who fatally shot a seventeen-year-old African American named Trayvon Martin in Sanford, Florida, where he was visiting his father. Born in 1995 a month after our boys were born, Trayvon was followed, shot, and killed by Zimmerman, who was acting as a "neighborhood watchman," because he thought Trayvon was suspicious. More than six weeks later, Zimmerman is finally arrested and ultimately tried for second-degree murder. He uses Florida's "Stand Your Ground" law as part of his defense. And he is acquitted.

Since Trayvon's murder, it has become painfully evident in case after case after case that police are gunning down unarmed African American men and women at an alarming rate, often without cause except for the fact that they're driving or walking or riding a bicycle "while Black." We need wholesale reform of our police departments.

*June 2012*

Carter's a junior, but he's taking Sarah Gruman, a senior, to her prom. They've been spending a lot of time together. By the time summer's over, they're "a couple." Even though they'll be separated in the fall—Sarah will be going to Columbia University's Barnard College in New York City and Carter will be a senior at Mira Costa High—they're planning how to make the separation work. Braden and Jackson have girlfriends, of course, but neither is in a "committed relationship" like this. Individuation?

*August 3, 2012*

Five o'clock in the morning on a warm August day following the boys' junior year, we're on our way to Los Angeles International Airport for a flight to New York. The guys are sixteen, and the five of us are embarking on a three-week college tour. It's a trip we can't afford to see colleges we can't afford. It's perfect.

As we head out, I'm remembering the year before I went to college. Seven months after I turned sixteen, President John F. Kennedy was assassinated in Dallas on November 22, 1963. I was a "Kennedy kid." I loved the Kingston Trio, the Beatles, the Beach Boys, and the Kennedys. I applied to Harvard, Yale, Stanford, and UC Berkeley, but I wanted to go to Harvard because John F. Kennedy went there. I dreamed of going into government service because of Kennedy. His death broke my world.

I did go to Harvard, very much trying to keep my dream alive. I worked summers in Washington, DC, for Congressman Lionel Van Deerlin (D-San Diego). I met Robert F. Kennedy in the courtyard of the Senate office building, overflowing with congressional interns who just wanted to see him up close and maybe touch him. As I shook Kennedy's hand, he said, "Hi, good of you to come." And then to the next intern, "Hi, good of you to come." I loved it.

Then, in February 1965, Muslim minister and civil rights leader Malcolm X was assassinated. It shook the world, and my world, but I kept going. I still envisioned working in government and eventually getting into politics.

In April 1968, just two months before I graduated, Martin Luther King Jr. was assassinated in Memphis, Tennessee. I was devastated. The world was devastated. It felt like the America I expected to grow up in was crumbling.

Then in June, as I was literally on the way to my Harvard graduation, Robert F. Kennedy was assassinated in Los Angeles. The day before, I had cast the first vote of my life, for RFK, in California's presidential primary, which he won.

I was heartbroken and disillusioned. It put out my fire.

I'm not proud of it, but with the Vietnam war still raging—a war I actively opposed—I wanted nothing to do with Washington, DC, the US government, or politics. Now, decades later, as we embark on our sons' college tour together, I wonder whether they will be confronted by challenges and disappointments during their college years that will cause them to change course.

## The Tour

We'll be out for three weeks because the guys are still playing baseball, and they've signed up to be seen at two camps that are more than two weeks apart. They (and we) think their athletic prowess could be a smart asset on their college applications, so rather than return to LA and go out again, we'll stay on the road.

We start at the Headfirst Honor Roll Camp in Yaphank on Long Island, a camp for ballplayers who want to attend top universities. Over two days, the boys are seen batting and playing in the field by coaches from leading colleges and universities including Stanford and MIT. The tryouts go well, but our kids say they feel "small" compared to sixteen and seventeen-year-olds from other parts of the country. Our boys aren't small, but they also don't look like they drove to camp and might have kids of their own. At one point, Jackson comes off the field and says, "Dad, the coaches can't even *see* us."

From Yaphank, we drive into Manhattan and take the train to Philadelphia. In Philly, we get a guided tour of the University of Pennsylvania and, at Jackson's insistence, visit the Barnes Museum, which turns out to be the highlight of our Penn visit. The next day, we take the train to Washington, DC, where we check out the monuments and receive a guided tour of the Capitol arranged by Representative Janice Hahn. The following day, as we tour Georgetown University, Braden says, "I don't want to go here. It looks like Hogwarts."

Everywhere we go, museum visits are high on Jackson's list; he has always had an eye and a passion for art, and we're grateful to him for adding to the visual richness of our trip. In DC, we visit the Smithsonian *and* the National Gallery of Art, which is showcasing the powerful work of George Bellows. Jackson is ecstatic.

By train and by car, we visit more schools chosen by the boys—the University of Virginia, Duke, and the University of North Carolina. At

UVA, of course, we visit the Fralin Museum of Art. At Duke, the boys think our guide is "hot." She's the daughter of one of my college classmates. Next, we fly to Boston and drive down to Cape Cod to take a break and watch the Cape Cod Baseball League playoffs. We know the coach of the Orleans Firebirds, Kelly Nicholson (he's from Manhattan Beach). It's a welcome "rest stop."

Since the boys will start applying to colleges when we get home, we've arranged for them to begin working on their essays with a counselor while we're traveling. One afternoon in Orleans, after they've each spent some time on the phone with their "essay coach," they start writing. Carter's essay will be titled "60 feet, 6 inches," the distance from the pitcher's mound to home plate. Braden will write about how his connection to the ocean and surfing has influenced his life. Jackson will write about making art, which he has been doing since middle school. When I ask them how they feel about starting their college essays, Braden says, "Dad, it's *Shark Week*." Apparently for the moment, they're more interested in the wildly popular TV series on Discovery.

The tour continues with Tufts, Boston College, and Harvard, where we get a guided tour of the campus prior to the boys reporting to the Harvard baseball camp. At the camp, they learn that Harvard's head coach, Joe Walsh, with whom they've been emailing, died suddenly at home on July 31, two weeks before the camp. Everyone is devastated by the news, and our guys are deeply disappointed they won't be meeting Coach Walsh.

From Boston, we drive to Providence to visit the Rhode Island School of Design—of interest to Jackson only—and Brown University. The next day, we fly to Detroit to visit the University of Michigan at Ann Arbor where Jackson has requested, and we receive, a guided tour of UM's impressive fine arts complex and art studios. From Detroit, we fly to St. Louis to visit Washington University, a beautiful campus at which Jackson has prearranged an "art interview." The boys have friends who are applying to Wash U., but they don't seem interested in coming here.

From St. Louis, we fly to Chicago for a visit to Northwestern and a guided tour of Obama Headquarters, which includes a brief meet and greet with David Axelrod, a senior adviser to the president who we first met in 2004 while campaigning for John Edwards. The headquarters, which occupies the entire floor of a high-rise building and is populated with dozens of young volunteers and staff members at computers, is impressive and a real eye-opener for the guys. As we leave, they're saying, "Obama's got this."

In the afternoon, we have a gentle sail on Lake Michigan with Barb's cousin, Deb Roberts, and her husband, Clinton, who expertly helms a sailboat they generously provide for the occasion. Our cruise concludes with a spectacular view of the city of Chicago lighting up as the sun sets on the lake. The next day, we attend a Rockies vs. Cubs game at Wrigley Field—a "bucket list" destination—before catching an evening flight home.

In many ways, the triplets' college tour represents a coming of age. Our sons learned how to travel; they learned what it takes to wake up in time to make an early flight, plow through airport ticketing and security, check in and out of hotels, rent cars, board trains, go sightseeing, tour museums, and snag a table for five when we wanted to eat. They started their college essays and got clearer about where they want to apply. They're getting ready for what's next. They're becoming young men.

## Spring 2012

Throughout their high school years, the boys are continuing to pursue their passion for baseball. As freshmen, they played on the same team and, during the summer before their sophomore year, they traveled the triumphant road to Bangor to play in the Senior Little League World Series. After a successful sophomore year together on the junior varsity team, they're learning, as juniors, that abuse doesn't come only from men and women exerting their power over others in social, business, or government settings. For too many boys and girls growing up, abuse can come in the form of a bad coach.

Braden and Jackson are playing on the JV team—Braden in the infield, Jackson in the outfield—while Carter, acknowledged to be a strong pitcher who can change speeds and locate the ball, is invited to "play up" with the varsity team. Having boys on both teams, we are in a unique position to see the impact of the two different coaches on players and parents. The JV coach is a teacher and an even-tempered baseball guy whose guidance is enabling the JV team and its players to thrive. The varsity coach who heads the program, also a teacher, is accused of being manipulative and a bully.

The coach's questionable behavior starts in the boys' sophomore year when he calls all the players in the program together during a practice, seats them in the bleachers, and launches an inquisition into allegations that certain players have been drinking and/or smoking pot on weekends. (The allegations do not involve behavior during school hours, on school property, or at school events off campus.) The coach passes out cards to the players and demands they write down the names of any of their fellow athletes who they know, or suspect, have been imbibing. The meeting, pitting players who are minors against each other, without any school officials present, is not only shocking and irresponsible but also probably illegal. It comes out that some of the players are writing down the names of other players, while others are refusing to go along. Our boys tell us later that they didn't write down any names.

Now, as their junior year gets going, a climate of fear and recrimination has infected the program; parents and players alike are afraid to come forward with complaints about the coach for fear their kids will be punished. The coach's conduct is becoming so outrageous that parents are demanding his removal for being a bully, an incompetent manager, and for violating provisions of the agreement he signed to serve as a coach. Thirty-seven parents accuse the coach of being physically, verbally, and mentally abusive to their children in the program. They detail their complaints in written statements, which are given unique numbers to protect the parents and players from retribution by the coach. The statements, which are collected and read by a retired judge, describe incidents in which players are berated, verbally attacked, humiliated in front of their teammates, and made to work out while injured. The judge says, in many cases, the experiences described are heartbreaking.

When the parents' complaints are presented to school officials, the principal and superintendent say they won't consider them because they're "anonymous," even though the judge and an attorney representing the parents say they know the names that go with the unique numbers. Numerous parents meet with the principal and superintendent in person to share their experiences and register their complaints, but still no action is taken. And now, those families are exposed. It gets so bad that three top players are transferring to other high schools—for their senior year—to escape abuse by the coach.

In the meantime, and these are mean times, the triplets are enduring different forms of treatment and mistreatment. Carter, who has been lured up to varsity to pitch, rarely plays. He has hit a home run on the school's largest field, but he is made a "pitcher only" and never allowed to bat again. He is simultaneously being sidelined by the coach and singled out for humiliation. In one particularly painful incident, the coach blindsides Carter with a verbal assault and then, as someone who maligns "quitters," tries to bait Carter into quitting. I pick the boys up from practice that day and, after we get home and his brothers have gone in the house, Carter stays in the car with me. And he breaks down, sobbing like he never has before, from deep down inside, injured not only by the incident with the coach but also the realization that his dream of playing baseball in high school is being shattered. And for no good reason.

*Fall 2013*

In the fall of the boys' senior year, allegations are still swirling around the baseball coach. Thus far, the superintendent and principal have repeatedly looked the other way. Now, they're conducting a lackadaisical "investigation" led by the athletic director and the vice principal to defend the errant coach's behavior. In "interviews" that were supposed to be anonymous but aren't, players feel intimidated about sharing their experiences, and if they do, they're discounted. For reasons no one understands, other than to dilute the responses, players who have never been on a team led by the accused coach are also being interviewed. Surprisingly, there is no one taking notes or recording the interviews. Not surprisingly, the resulting report is a whitewash.

The principal's summary says the investigation determined that the coach caused student athletes to ignore written medical directives from their physicians; offered players incentives in exchange for raising funds for the baseball booster club, placing the district in a position of liability; and engaged in a pattern of conduct that created an unhealthy fear of the coach. While claiming "There is no evidence indicating physical, mental, or emotional abuse," the principal's summary conveniently ignores the numerous written and in-person statements from parents to the contrary. When the coach puts the senior team together, he includes Carter and Braden but cuts Jackson, after Barbara and I have shown support for the group seeking the coach's removal. I realize many parents who think the coach should be removed are keeping their mouths shut to protect their kids. Sometimes, I wish we had done that. Jackson is a superb baseball player—disciplined, positive, coachable, talented in the outfield, "clutch" at bat—all words I've heard coaches and other dads use to describe him. He was co-captain of the JV team; he had a twelve-game hitting streak and the second highest batting average on the team, second only to Braden. In strictly baseball terms, Jackson deserves to be on the varsity team with his brothers. But the coach is telling him, "I don't go by stats" when, of course, baseball is all about stats. He's also telling Jackson he wants to "limit the size of the team" this year and yet is including a player who recently had Tommy John surgery and won't play all season. It's clear: cutting Jackson is retribution, plain and simple.

As the season begins, Carter is being targeted in subtle and not-so-subtle ways. He realizes he will not be allowed to play and is facing another year of mistreatment at the hands of the coach. Knowing the coach's reputation for bad-mouthing players who quit, Carter comes up with the idea of asking the coach for a "mutual release" whereby, if he leaves the team, the coach will not say anything negative about him and he will not say anything about the coach. In a fraught meeting with our family, we are witness to the angry, abusive, and manipulative behavior for which the coach has been accused. When Carter asks for the mutual release, the coach is suspicious until one of his enablers tells him, "It's okay, Coach. It's not a trap. He wants to play club ball." After the meeting, Carter gathers his teammates and tells them he's leaving the team. It's a courageous and forthright move. Braden cries at the meeting, saying later, "I couldn't believe an outside force could break the seemingly unbreakable bond between me and my brothers."

Braden, a five-tool player who can hit, run, hit for power, field, and throw, remains on the team but, ironically, is never coached by the accused bully. The constant flood of accusations is finally catching up with the coach. For the first half of the season, the coach is suspended and banned from having anything to do with the team. Braden and his teammates resolve to play for each other; they make it to the California Interscholastic Federation (CIF) finals at Dodger Stadium, where Braden hits a double, bringing in his team's only run.

Despite all that's happened, Barbara volunteers to help organize the baseball banquet at the end of the season. "It's one of the hardest things I've ever done," she says later. "With two of our sons excluded, it's painful to work through." And guess what? When the coaches introduce the players who are honored, all they talk about are their stats.

High school baseball taught our boys that not all adults are good people and not all coaches know what they're doing. It was a surprising revelation for them. Across a dozen years, our sons were coached by at least thirty-seven different men (we counted) with different personalities, backgrounds, strategies, standards, and expectations. But until now, all their coaches had one thing in common: they had integrity; they treated their players fairly and with respect, and they took responsibility for the experience their players had on and off the field. A bad coach can claim innocence and say he did nothing wrong, but he can't change the experience our sons had. The experiences they've had with this one coach is leaving scars.

(Ultimately, the baseball coach was disciplined by the State of California, his teaching credential suspended and nearly revoked when he refused to accept the suspension. But as is often the case with abuse, the remedy came too late to salvage what could have been—and should have been—a positive high school experience for a lot of fine athletes.)

## Spring 2013

The triplets applied to several colleges together, including Harvard, the University of California at Berkeley, the University of Virginia, Stanford, Tufts, Oberlin, Duke, and the University of Michigan. Jackson has applied to UCLA in the Art Department. We find out later that, just before the December 31 midnight deadline, Carter also applied on his own to Yale, NYU, and Cornell without telling us. As a Harvard man, I took his application to Yale personally until I realized all of Carter's last-minute school choices were in or near New York City so he could be close to Sarah.

Now, the guys are receiving their college acceptances. All three have been accepted at Berkeley, several other UC schools, the University of Virginia, and Oberlin, which wants them to play baseball. Jackson has been accepted at UCLA in the Art Department, an acknowledgement of his talent and a real feather in his cap. Braden and Jackson have gone for an overnight visit at Berkeley; Braden enjoyed it, but Jackson didn't. During spring break, Jackson visits UVA, hosted by a former classmate from Mira Costa; he's enthralled with UVA and convinces Braden they should go there. Meanwhile, Carter has been admitted to Cornell University, only four hours by bus from Sarah in New York City. Our kids have worked hard and been admitted to great schools. We couldn't be prouder.

*June 25, 2013*

A few days after our kids collect their high school diplomas and shake off their senior year of high school baseball, the Supreme Court is effectively striking down the heart of the Voting Rights Act of 1965. Wait, is this the world we're sending our children into?

By a 5-to-4 vote, the court's action frees nine states, mostly in the South, to change their election laws without advance federal approval. As Adam Liptak reported in the *New York Times*, "The court divided along ideological lines, and the two sides drew sharply different lessons from the history of the civil rights movement and the nation's progress in rooting out racial discrimination in voting. At the core of the disagreement was whether racial minorities continued to face barriers to voting in states with a history of discrimination." It's abundantly clear to us that they do. Indeed, in many places in today's America, schemes to limit access to voting and disenfranchise voters, especially voters of color, are threatening to destroy democracy.

Clearly, the right to vote is fundamental, and every public official I can think of, from dog catcher to school board member and sheriff, is elected by the popular vote. *Except for our president.* For ridiculously archaic reasons, in presidential contests, it's not the popular vote that counts; it's the Electoral College vote that matters. And yet, in every presidential campaign I can remember before 2000—Kennedy, Johnson, Nixon, Carter, Bush #1, Clinton—the winner of the Electoral College vote and the winner of the popular vote were one and the same. Until Bush v. Gore in 2000. Gore received five hundred thousand more popular votes than Bush, but "W" became president anyway thanks to the Supreme Court and the Electoral College, which is, after all, nothing more than an anachronistic institutional end run around the popular vote. ("W" is the first president our sons were aware of; Obama was the first president they "knew;" Hillary Clinton was the first presidential candidate they got to vote for. In 2016, Hillary received three million more popular votes nationwide than reality show host Donald Trump. Still, by dint of gathering just seventy-seven thousand more votes than Clinton across three battleground states, Trump captured the Electoral College and became president. Like W, Trump was not America's popular choice.)

Polls consistently show that most Americans favor replacing the Electoral College with a nationwide popular vote. And the good news is—we can. While everyone agrees it would be incredibly difficult to pass a constitutional amendment to abolish the Electoral College, there is a work-around.

In January 2006, when our kids were in fifth grade, a brilliant idea came into existence that, all these years later, can transform our electoral system. It's called the National Popular Vote Interstate Compact (NPVIC). The NPVIC will guarantee the presidency to the candidate who receives the most popular votes across all fifty states and the District of Columbia. The compact is a state-based approach that preserves the Electoral College, state control of elections, and the power of the states to control how the president is elected. At the same time, it ensures that *every* vote, in *every* state, will matter in *every* presidential election.

The National Popular Vote bill will take effect when enacted by states with a combined total of 270 electoral votes, the number of Electoral College votes needed to become president. As of April 2021, the compact had been adopted by fifteen states and the District of Columbia. These states have 196 electoral votes between them, which is 73 percent of the 270 votes needed to give the compact legal force. Included are four small states (Delaware, Hawaii, Rhode Island, Vermont), eight medium-size states (Colorado, Connecticut, Maryland, Massachusetts, New Jersey, New Mexico, Oregon, Washington), three big states (California, Illinois, New York), and the District of Columbia.

The bill only needs states with a total of 74 more electoral votes between them to become operative. The NPVIC has passed at least one chamber (assembly or senate) in nine additional states, which have a total of 88 electoral votes between them (Arkansas, Arizona, Maine, Michigan, Minnesota, North Carolina, Nevada, Oklahoma, Virginia), so success is within reach. Moreover, adding to the possibility of passage is the fact that in 2020, the Biden-Harris ticket won in states that haven't signed on to the NPVIC but have 79 electoral votes between them: Georgia (16), Arizona (11), Nevada (6), Michigan (16), Pennsylvania (20), and Wisconsin (10). These states would seem to be achievable targets that could make the NPVIC a reality by 2028 and possibly even in time for the 2024 presidential election. Enactment of the National Popular Vote Interstate Compact is within reach.

(Patriotic plug: To volunteer, donate, or offer your support, contact National Popular Vote https://www.nationalpopularvote.com/ or write to Maryland Congressman Jamie Raskin, one of the original architects of the compact, at 2242 Rayburn House Office Building, Washington, DC 20515.)

*Our Greatest Challenge*

As our sons head off to college and I prepare to empty my IRA to help pay for tuitions, the existential crisis created by climate change is upon us. Everyone reading this book will be dealing with it during their lifetimes. Most Americans have already experienced climate change where they live in the form of increasingly violent storms, raging wildfires, unforeseen flooding, sea level rise, crop failures, drought, and unseasonal temperatures. And there's more to come. The climate emergency will cause massive migrations that will upend global stability. Warming is already affecting food production and water supplies. Sea level rise is already destroying property and property values in various parts of the world, including Florida and the Gulf Coast, while threatening to displace millions around the world who live at the ocean's edge. And yet the kind of global World War II-scale mobilization needed to address the climate emergency across the planet has not been mounted. To quote Greta Thunberg, the young Swedish environmental activist, "If we start treating the climate crisis like a crisis, that could change everything overnight."

The foundation for the climate crisis was laid in my father's America with the industrialization of the United States and a post-World War II explosion in the extraction and burning of fossil fuels. That's when we really started buying into the idea that the Earth was humankind's to plunder. That's also when the oil and gas industry began lying to protect that idea. Our reliance on burning fossil fuels continued unabated in the America my brothers and I grew up in, even though energy companies like Exxon Mobil and Shell knew in the 1970s that their products were contributing to global warming that would have dire consequences in the future. If you're thinking greed may have played a role in their deception, you're right.

Now, continuing to burn fossil fuels is pushing Earth ever closer to a temperature from which there will be no retreat or recourse. If we are to avoid a future disrupted by the devastating effects of global warming, climate scientists warn that we must keep the temperature of the planet from increasing by more than 1.5 degrees Celsius above Earth's average temperature of 15 degrees Celsius before the Industrial Revolution (1760-1840). In other words, if the Earth's average global land and ocean surface temperature reaches 16.5 degrees Celsius, conditions will become dire for *all* living things on large portions of the planet. Even small, incremental temperature increases will cause and are causing havoc—melting of ice caps, thawing of frozen tundra, rising sea levels. And scientists promise that without dramatic action, global warming is likely to increase by 1.5 degrees Celsius above preindustrial levels sometime between 2030 and 2052, with their best estimate being 2040.

So there's a clock on this.

I invite skeptics who doubt the significance of a 1.5-degree Celsius increase in Earth's rising temperature to think about it in terms of their own temperature. Even though we measure the planet's temperature in Celsius and our body temperature in Fahrenheit, incremental increases can be hugely significant. At 98.6 degrees Fahrenheit, you feel fine. You're normal. But small increases in Fahrenheit can cause you to feel unwell. At 100 degrees Fahrenheit, an increase of just 1.4 degrees, you feel unwell, and you're probably becoming concerned. If your temperature climbs to 103 degrees, another small increase, you're in bed and on the phone to your doctor. If your temperature reaches 104 degrees, you're on your way to urgent care or the ER.

The science is clear: global warming is caused by human activity, and it's not something we can tolerate, even in small amounts. Still, there are those who want to privatize government agencies rather than empower them to meet this moment; there are those who want to further deregulate the corporate sector rather than inspire it to be part of the solution; there are those who want to lower taxes for the largest corporations and richest Americans so they can continue fiddling while our planet burns instead of paying their fair share to meet the emergency. Said another way, the greatest threats to our survival on planet Earth are inaction and the scourge often cited in these pages: *greed*.

The intention of this book has been to share some of the most enlightening and memorable reflections from our adventure raising triplets while also alerting readers to how the America our triplets are inheriting has changed along the way—not entirely for the better.

The America my father grew up in wasn't perfect, and the America my brothers and I came up in wasn't perfect either. But for my parents and much of my life, it felt like the American dream was alive and well for a lot of people. Now, it feels like the American dream is functionally beyond the reach of most people. This condition is unsustainable. We need a new version of American capitalism for the twenty-first century that embodies diversity, equity, and inclusion and, most urgently, will enable us to meet and survive the climate emergency. The time to create that new capitalism is now.

It's time to be greater, more generous, more loving, respectful, responsible, and kind as we meet the enormous challenges before us. We learned this from raising triplet boys: Don't panic. Take one day at a time. Stay committed. Don't give up.

# EPILOGUE

While sorting through some photos for this book, I found a letter addressed to our boys dated September 18, 1997. They were two and half years old. I never gave them the letter. If I had, they wouldn't have been able to read it. What I realized, as I read it all these years later, is that I must have been afraid. Afraid that something would take me from them. Afraid of dying. I must have been thinking, if anything should happen to me, I want my sons to have this expression of my hopes for them and my unconditional love for them. They have the letter now, and I wouldn't change a word.

*September 18, 1997*

*Dear Carter, Braden & Jackson:*
*We don't know how much time we will have together. I'm committed that it will be many, many joyful years. And I pray that I will be around to sing (whether you like it or not) at each of your respective weddings.*

*There is a quote I love that I would like you to remember:*

> ***"The past is history. The future is a mystery.
> And the present is a gift."***

*I love this quote because it speaks to how important it is to enjoy each and every moment in life. And I want you to know that, whatever happens, I regard every moment spent with each of you boys as a precious gift that can never be taken from us.*

*I also want you to remember something that Deepak Chopra says in his book,* The Seven Spiritual Laws of Success*:*

*You each have a unique talent and a unique way of expressing it. There is something that each of you can do better than anyone else in the whole world—and for every unique talent and every unique expression of that talent, there are also unique needs.*

*When these needs are matched with the creative expression of your talent, that is the spark that creates affluence. Expressing your talents to fulfill needs creates unlimited wealth, abundance, and satisfaction.*

*I also want to say to you what Deepak Chopra said to his children:*

*I never, ever want you to worry about making a living. If you're unable to make a living when you grow up, your Mother and I, or what we leave behind, will provide for you, so don't worry about that.*

*I don't want you to worry about doing well in school. I don't want you to worry about getting the best grades or going to the best colleges.*

# EPILOGUE

*What I really want you to focus on is asking yourself how you can serve humanity and asking yourself what your unique talents are. Because each of you—Carter, Braden & Jackson—has a unique talent that no one else has, and you have a special way of expressing that talent, and no one else has it.*

*If you focus on what you are here to give, you will get the best grades, go to the best colleges and be financially self-sufficient.*

*I love you deeply, completely, and unconditionally. And my love will always be here for you. Take care of each other,*

*— Your Father*

The triplets went off to college in the fall of 2013. After they left, the house was suddenly so quiet, so still, that we bought a couple of tumbleweeds so there would be something moving. It felt like the jobs we had for eighteen years ended, but there was no retirement party, and neither of us received a gold watch.

Still, we felt an enormous sense of accomplishment and pride that our sons were on their way to what author Gail Sheehy years ago dubbed "provisional adulthood." At one point, before Braden and Jackson went off to the University of Virginia (UVA), I said to Braden, "Maybe your mom and I will buy a place in Charlottesville so we'll have a place to stay when we come to the East Coast to visit you guys." To which Braden replied, with a devilish grin, "Dad, we're going to school on the East Coast to get away from you." Barbara took the guys to their respective colleges—Braden and Jackson to UVA in Charlottesville, Virginia, and

Carter to Cornell in Ithaca, New York. I had just finished producing the American Film Institute (AFI) tribute to Mel Brooks in June, and in July-August was prepping the *2013 Humanitas Prize Awards* for mid-September. Thank you, Barbara, for escorting our sons on that long, tiring, and emotional journey with such grace and good humor.

The rest, as they say, is and will be the triplets' history:

Braden graduated from the University of Virginia in 2017 with a degree in finance from the undergraduate McIntire School of Commerce. Fun fact: Braden was invited to join UVA's varsity baseball team mid-season in 2015, the year UVA won the College World Series, but he declined the offer to avoid upending his class schedule and concentrate on his studies. After graduation, he worked at Wells Fargo for a year and Goldman Sachs for two years before becoming an associate with TPG Private Equity in San Francisco. Braden is a surfer, golfer, and an avid reader.

Sarah transferred from Columbia Barnard to Cornell in the spring of 2014; Carter and Sarah were married that summer. Their daughter, Ruth, was born in September 2015. They both graduated from Cornell in 2016, Carter with a BS degree in Policy Analysis and Management and Sarah with a degree in Human Development. Carter went on to earn a master's degree in Civil and Environmental Engineering from Stanford University (2017); their second daughter, Tova, was born in 2018, and Carter earned a PhD in Civil and Environmental Engineering from Stanford in 2019. Shortly after their third daughter, Ella, was born, they moved to England, where Carter spent a year as a lecturer in economics and finance at the University College of London's Bartlett School of Construction and Project Management. In 2021, Carter, Sarah and their three girls moved back to the US so Carter could explore opportunities at Stanford and Cornell.

Jackson graduated from the University of Virginia in 2017 with a dual degree in Fine Art and Marketing, the latter from the McIntire

School of Commerce. After college, Jackson, a painter, worked out of his own studio in Inglewood, California, for two years. He had his first solo show in 2020 at the Richard Heller Gallery in Santa Monica, at the height of the COVID-19 pandemic. He sold *all* the paintings in the show plus several from inventory which gallerist Heller called "a truly auspicious beginning for a new artist." Jackson's work can be seen at www.jacksoncasady.com or on Instagram @jacksoncasady. He now lives and paints in a studio in the Arts District in downtown Los Angeles. Jackson is a surfer, screenwriter, and student of the fine arts.

## *The Lottery*

I used to wonder what it would be like to win the lottery. The day you win, you'd be thrilled beyond belief, of course. Then the next day, when you woke up, you'd realize, *Hey, I won the lottery yesterday!* And it wouldn't stop. Every day thereafter, you'd still be a lottery winner. How amazing would that be?

On January 7, 1995, when our triplets were born healthy and whole, we won the *baby lottery*. And the next day, the feeling was still there. The reality was there. *They* were there.

And it hasn't stopped. We get to live with it every day. Through all the years, all the phases and stages, challenges and accomplishments, we've been blessed to live with the enormous, priceless gift and source of pride that our triplet sons are to us every single day. And now, these spectacular young adults are creating their own lives, careers, families, and the future.

I used to wonder what it would be like to win the lottery.

Now, I know.

1995, Age 6 months.
Left to right: Jackson,
Braden, Carter

1996, Age 1 year. Left to right: Carter, Jackson, Braden

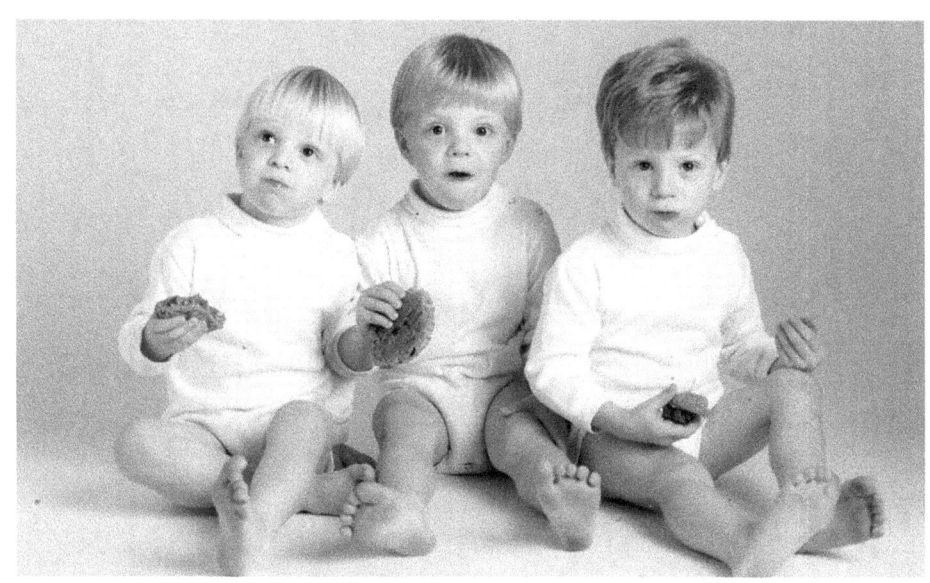

1997, Age 2½. Left to right: Braden, Carter, Jackson — *Photo by Curtis Dahl*

2000, Age 5.
Top to bottom:
Jackson, Carter, Braden
— *Photo by Curtis Dahl*

2005, Age 10. Left to right: Carter, Barbara, Braden, Cort, and Jackson — *Photo by Curtis Dahl*

2006, Age 11. Left to right: Carter, Cort, Barbara, Braden, and Jackson — *Photo by Curtis Dahl*

2006, Age 11, Encino Little League. Left to right: Braden, Carter, Jackson

2011, Age 16. Jackson, Braden, Carter

2010, Age 15. Left to right: Carter, Jackson, Braden, Cort and Barbara.

2011, Age 16. Jackson batting.

2011, Age 16. Carter pitching.

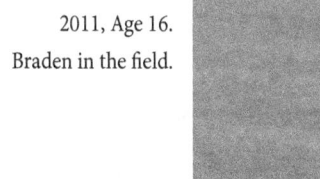

2011, Age 16, Casady family. Left to right: Jackson, Cort, Barbara, Carter, Braden

2016, Age 21. Left to right: Braden, Jackson, Carter — *Photo by Curtis Dahl*

# ABOUT THE AUTHOR

CORT CASADY has won two Emmy Awards and three NAACP Image Awards for his work as a television and documentary writer-producer. He won his first Emmy for *New York at Night Starring Clint Holmes*, a daily, live, prime time variety-talk series he created for Superstation WWOR-New York (1992). He won his second Emmy for the *American Film Institute (AFI) Life Achievement Award: A Tribute to Mel Brooks* (2014). His numerous credits include creating the original story and characters for the five-installment TV movie mini-series *Kenny Rogers as The Gambler*, helping to format and launch the long-running reality competition series, *Star Search* with Ed McMahon, a forerunner of *American Idol*, and co-creating television's first weekly environmental series. Launched as *Earthbeat*, the series aired as *Network Earth* on TBS for five years.

Since 2003, Cort has served as supervising producer of the annual *American Film Institute (AFI) Life Achievement Award* tributes to America's leading actors and filmmakers. He has also written and produced televised music-documentary tributes to R&B legends Quincy Jones, Stevie Wonder (2007 Image Award winner), Aretha Franklin, Smokey Robinson

(2009 Image Award winner), Patti LaBelle, Lionel Richie (2011 Image Award winner), and Chaka Khan.

Cort is the coauthor of two published books: *The Singing Entertainer* (with John Davidson, Alfred Publishing, 1979), a handbook for professional singers, and *You Oughta Be Me: How to Be a Lounge Singer and Live Like One* by the Fabulous Bud E. Luv (with Ned Claflin, St. Martin's Press, 1993), a humorus faux autobiography. Casady is the coauthor with Mary Miller of the musical play *King of the Road: The Roger Miller Story*, which had its world premiere at the Laguna Playhouse in Laguna Beach, California, in 2017.

Cort began his show business career as a commercial coordinator at KNBC-TV in Burbank prior to becoming a production assistant on the *Smothers Brothers Comedy Hour*; he was subsequently made vice president of the Los Angeles production of the rock musical *Hair* because he was the only person in the company with a clean police record. He then joined veteran personal manager Ken Kragen in a management and production company representing Kenny Rogers, Mason Williams, Jennifer Warnes, John Hartford, and John Stewart. Cort left artist management to become an investigative magazine writer, author, songwriter, and television writer-producer.

www.ingramcontent.com/pod-product-compliance
Lightning Source LLC
LaVergne TN
LVHW010201070526
838199LV00062B/4454